Chartering a Boat

Chartering a Boat

Your Guide to a Perfect Holiday

Chris Caswell

SHERIDAN HOUSE

This book is dedicated to my wife, Rhea. She's the best crew, navigator, chef, and companion a man could have, and I can't imagine chartering with anyone else. She's a stern taskmaster when it comes to making me meet deadlines, and she threatens to lock me in my office, withholding lunch, until I hand her a finished chapter. But she puts umbrellas in my drinks when we're anchored, she's never shown fear even when my knuckles are white, and I look forward to exploring the world's charter paradises with her. She doesn't travel light, but she travels well. Thanks for the memories.

First published 2001 by
Sheridan House Inc.
145 Palisade Street
Dobbs Ferry, NY 10522

Library of Congress Cataloging-in-Publication Data

Caswell, Christopher.
Chartering a boat : your guide to a perfect holiday / Chris Caswell.
p. cm.
Includes bibliographical references (p.) and index.
ISBN 1-57409-111-5 (alk. paper)
1. Boats and boating—Chartering. 2. Seamanship. 3. Yachting. I. Title.

GV775 .C337 2001
797.1'246—dc21

2001020130

Edited by Janine Simon
Production management by Quantum Publishing Services, Inc., Bellingham, Washington
Designed by Jill S. Mathews
Photos by the author unless otherwise noted

Printed in the United States of America

ISBN 1-57409-111-5

Part I—The Basics

Chapter	1	What's It All About?	3
	2	Choosing a Charter Area	17
	3	Choosing a Charter Company	23
	4	Selecting a Boat	31
	5	Catamarans	45
	6	Powerboat Charters	51
	7	Picking Your Crew	61
	8	Paperwork	65
	9	What to Take	73
	10	Tips on Saving Dollars	79

Part II—The Skills

Chapter	11	Seamanship	85
	12	Anchoring	93
	13	Navigation	103
	14	Dinghies	109
	15	Safety and First Aid	117
	16	Provisioning	127
	17	Living Aboard	137

Part III—Charter Areas

Chapter	18	The Caribbean	147
	19	The Bahamas and North America	159
	20	Europe	175
	21	The South Pacific and Asia	189
		Appendix 1: Charter Seasons	205
		Appendix 2: Checklists	207
		Further Reading	209
		Index	213

Part I
The Basics

1

What's It All About?

It was a pristine morning, clear and bright, with the promise of an afternoon breeze to balance the sun's warmth. Padding quietly up the cabin steps into the cockpit, I settled back against a cushion and wiggled my toes with pleasure on the cool deck. Just off our stern, wavelets rushed up the white sand beach with a soft shushing sound, and the green palms sparkled silver with dew in the faint tropical breeze.

A rich man at play? Hardly. This was simply another morning aboard a charter yacht, anchored in a quiet cove that could be anywhere in the world. Where the pleasures of Tahiti, the Virgin Islands, and the Mediterranean coast were once the private playground of the very wealthy, today's boater can sample any of them on an average vacation budget.

The first myth that must be dispensed with is that chartering a yacht is an expensive proposition. In fact, the price is comparable to what you might expect to pay at a good resort hotel with few of the pleasures to be found on your own yacht.

As an example, let's look at a 38-foot yacht in the British Virgin Islands. This particular yacht, typical of those available at many charter companies, has three separate cabins, two private head compartments with showers, and a dinette that converts into another double berth, giving a total sleeping capacity of eight adults. But, for the sake of this comparison, let's say that you want the maximum of privacy so only two couples are going to charter this yacht.

With powerful winches and wide decks, this Moorings 500 is a pleasure to sail. (Courtesy of The Moorings.)

In the January to April high season, when most visitors schedule their vacations to escape from the winter chill of northern climates, the yacht charters for about $4200 per week, or $2100 per couple.

A first rate Caribbean resort hotel would charge at least $300 per night in the same area, so the basic cost is essentially equal. In a hotel, however, the meals are going to be a major factor in your budget. A basic breakfast can easily run $15 a person (and that isn't for room service), while sandwiches, salad and wine for lunch can exceed $20. A week of simple meals in a hotel can set you back $800 per couple, which is far more than you'll be paying for provisions aboard a charter yacht.

Besides, in a hotel you have the choice of waiting in line for a seat in the dining room or splurging on room service. Aboard your yacht, you can choose between a meal al fresco with a spectacular view, or you can take breakfast back into your cabin for a lazy morning. Even if you leave your yacht to dine ashore every evening, your total vacation costs are going to be lower than in the resort hotel. So what's holding you back?

You'll have a wide latitude of boats to choose among, and we'll look at the various types and some of the decisions you'll make later in this book.

The price of a charter yacht is directly proportional to the quality and maintenance level of the yacht, the sea-

The well-protected harbor of Anse Marcel on St. Martin has several charter bases and a resort so charterers can arrive early or stay late.

son, and the size of the charter company. Large charter operations, such as The Moorings, are able to keep their prices down because of their buying power and by employing a full-time maintenance staff which, in turn, means the boats are in premium condition. A one-boat charter company, on the other hand, may be able to charge lower rates but would be unable to provide either the quality or the reliability.

CAN YOU SAIL?

The basic prerequisite for bareboat chartering is that you know how to sail or, in the case of a powerboat, know how to operate such a yacht. Charter yachts, regardless of their size, are valuable and you'll be responsible for the safety of the yacht and the crew, so you should have a good working knowledge of boating. Bareboat chartering is not for the rank amateur, and you'll need to have both boating ability and some cruising experience before you cast off on your own.

The skills you'll need, however, are dependent upon where you plan to charter. In the British Virgin Islands, for example, there are few underwater hazards, no fog, and the sailing area is just 36 miles long, so you navigate by eye rather than relying on chart skills. If you plan to tackle a more challenging area, however, you'll need more than rudimentary sailing and boat handling to see you through.

Don't try to skate by with marginal skills, because charter companies are expert at ferreting out imposters, both from the sailing experience questionnaire and when they put you to the acid test with a check-out on their boat. You can avoid a lot of grief, as well as a possibly ruined vacation, by being coldly analytical about your own abilities beforehand.

On the positive side, don't be put off just because your experience lies in small boats rather than yachts of charter boat proportions. If you sail centerboard boats regularly, you'll have a good feel for sailing even if you're weak in big boat handling, which you can pick up quickly in many of the milder chartering locales.

To encourage new charterers, The Moorings has a "Friendly Skipper" program where they will provide you with a skipper for two days to get you started on your charter and to make sure you understand everything necessary. The only cost (aside from the charter itself) is the return fare for the skipper to his base of operations. You can expect other charter companies to follow suit with similar offers for first-timers.

One thing that is very useful is to have decision-making experience aboard boats of similar size to your charter boat, rather than just time as a crewmember. Simply sitting as "deck fluff" doesn't qualify you as a skipper.

GAINING EXPERIENCE

There are several ways to gain the experience and skills necessary for bareboat chartering: sail locally with friends, take courses at a sailing school, sign on for a flotilla charter, or sail as crew on a charter.

If you're interested in sailing, you're probably friendly with boat owners, and now is the time to ask for their help. As sailors, they know how difficult it can be to learn sailing, and nearly every skipper is glad to help novices. Under their supervision, practice docking and anchoring, or see if they'll let you be the "skipper for the day," with responsibility for all aspects of the day sail. While this is the most convenient and least expensive way to learn to sail, it is dependent upon the skills of your friends as instructors. Just as one member of your family may not be the best to teach others in the family to drive, the same holds true in sailing. Putting aside the egos and the psychological baggage of being someone's student, your friends simply may not be capable of teaching you.

In many cases, your best choice is to sign up with a sailing school, which will probably have a wide range of courses from basic sailing all the way through celestial navigation. In between, you're likely to find courses to help hone your charter cruising skills such as anchoring, boat handling, and basic navigation.

TYPES OF CHARTERS

Before you sign up for a charter, you'll need to decide which style of charter best fits your needs. In general, there are six different types of yacht charters:

1. Bareboat
2. Crewed
3. Flotilla
4. School
5. Special Interest
6. Head boats

These aren't hard and fast categories and, as the charter industry expands worldwide, you're more likely to find combinations and even new gimmicks to entice you. Let's take a look at the six basic charters.

Bareboating

Bareboat charters are the most popular, and you'll find fleets of bareboat charter yachts worldwide. "Bareboat" doesn't mean clothing optional, however, but means that the yacht is supplied to you without a crew. You and your crew will operate the yacht, doing everything from hoisting and trimming sail to anchoring at day's end. You do the sailing, cooking, and cleaning. All of the challenges, and all of the rewards, are yours.

You'll be able to decide where to go each day, when to anchor, and when to linger. On the other hand, you'll be assuming responsibility for the yacht, so you'll need to exercise both skill and caution in your actions.

But don't let that scare you off. Each charter company carefully checks you out on the boat, assessing your skills while they show you how everything works on board. You'll probably be asked to take one of their staff for a spin around the harbor to test your boat handling skills as well.

Before you leave the dock on your first day, you'll get an extensive briefing that will answer all your questions about the sailing area. Using charts like those supplied on your boat, a member of the charter company team will show you which are the best anchorages, what hazards to watch for, as well as provide details on everything from weather to sightseeing to restaurants.

Bareboating has become an alternative to yacht ownership for many former boat owners, who found the expenses outweighed the pleasures of owning their boats. As one experienced bareboat sailor noted, "Bareboat chartering is like being a grandparent: you get the pleasures when you want them, for as long as you want them, but with none of the responsibilities!"

Besides, the average boat owner has neither the time nor the money to sail over the horizon to faraway places. By chartering a bareboat yacht, he can simply climb on a jet and, in a few hours, be in Tahiti, Thailand, the French West Indies, or the Greek archipelago. As one bareboater pointed out, "I'm simply sailing around the world....one piece at a time."

Crewed Charters

While most people think of crewed charters as being the province of Lifestyles of the Rich and Famous, that simply isn't the case. For every 175-foot mega-yacht that is chartered by jetsetters for $20,000 a day including a full complement of uniformed crewmembers, there are dozens (perhaps hundreds) of 50- and 60-footers, run by husband-wife crews in casual clothing, that are chartered by average people.

The simplest form of crewed chartering is where only a skipper joins you aboard your boat. At most bareboat charter companies, you can hire a skipper to help you learn the ropes or explore an unfamiliar area. After a day or two, the skipper departs, leaving you to enjoy a bareboat charter for the remainder of your vacation. Depending on the cruising area, a short-term skipper can range from $50 to $125 a day, plus the cost of return transportation to the starting point.

For many charterers, having a professional skipper aboard is a relief from any worries about navigation, anchoring, docking, or the myriad little stresses of being entirely on your own. At the same time, a skipper can provide a valuable introduction into a new cruising area, giving a sense of security for future bareboat cruises in the same area.

A second form of crewed charter involves taking along a cook on your bareboat to handle all the galley chores. Every charter company can provide you with a choice, usually ranging from a Cordon Bleu-trained chef to a local cook who takes pride in preparing native fares. A cook handles the shopping, cooking, serving and clean-up for your meals, but this is for the galley only. You're on your own for keeping the rest of the boat clean.

By far the most common crewed charter, however, is the husband-wife team that operates their own yacht as a full-time business. In most cases, the husband is the skipper, while the wife acts as chef, stewardess and deckhand.

In this situation, you'll usually be allowed to do as much or as little as you choose, either leaving the boat's handling to the crew or taking an active part. The crew prepares the meals (working from a menu agreed upon beforehand), and usually handles the physical work such as furling the sails, anchoring, or launching the dinghy.

While the skipper may veto an idea because of danger, you'll be allowed to choose when and where you go; dallying in spots that you enjoy and upping-anchor from those that you don't care about.

Flotilla Charters

The flotilla charter is an idea that began in Europe and has now spread to charter fleets worldwide, although you'll still find far more flotillas scheduled in the Mediterranean and Aegean than anywhere else.

A flotilla charter is a group cruise of several charter boats, usually similar in size or speed, shepherded along by a mother ship with a professional captain from the charter company. This is the "buddy system" of boating. With some flotilla charters, the individual boats are free to sail alone during the day, choosing their route and stops, but anchoring together at an agreed-upon harbor each night. Other flotillas sail as a group, sometimes having races between the boats, but staying within sight of each other.

A flotilla is a comfortable combination of bareboat and crewed chartering, providing advice, camaraderie and any needed parts or repairs as the trip progresses. It's obviously less stressful on each skipper, since the mother ship keeps an eye on the flock, and it's an excellent way for those with less sailing experience to acquire new skills in a controlled environment.

With most flotillas, there is a predeparture briefing each morning for the crews, covering the day's route as well as sights and hazards in the area. With a conventional bareboat charter, the briefing covers an entire week or more, which is often hard to absorb, while the flotilla concentrates on just one day at a time.

A flotilla charter may also get better moorings as a group, and the charter company often has more clout in local harbors so dinner reservations, groceries and sightseeing are often easier than if you were bareboating on your own.

The negative side to a flotilla charter is that you aren't as free to plan your own itinerary, and must work with a large number of people to agree on all the details. Flotilla charters are often used by yacht clubs or other groups with similar interests.

I recently enjoyed a flotilla charter in Tahiti, using three Beneteau 51s and a Privilege 48 catamaran as the mother ship. Ours was a loose arrangement, agreeing each morning on where we would rendezvous that day, and amending our plans by radio as weather or personal inclinations changed.

On some days, we sailed from island to island in solitude, gathering aboard the mother catamaran in the evening for cocktails and socializing. Other days, we would agree to meet at a particular motu (islet) for swimming and lunch before proceeding at our own pace to the night's anchorage. The crew aboard the catamaran, with their local knowledge, were able to suggest the best beaches, coves and restaurants, but the crews were free to decide what they wanted to do. I had thought that I might feel confined by the bus tour mentality of following another boat around, but found that it was quite a pleasant way to explore a new area without worrying about charts, weather reports, or guide books.

Sailing Schools

A relatively new twist in chartering are the packages offered by sailing schools, which combine the pleasures of bareboating with a learning experience to improve your skills. These are usually flotilla charters, sometimes with a mother ship but more often with a skipper/instructor assigned to each boat.

Each school structures its program differently, but most start with a classroom session that covers the area to be sailed as well as details about the local weather. Once aboard the boats, each crew is responsible for running the boat under the guidance of the instructor, who only steps in when necessary. The crews rotate positions to learn the intricacies of steering, navigation, docking, anchoring and even cooking aboard.

Usually the only requirement for such a course is a knowledge of the basics of sailing, since the intent is to learn

Using a charter yacht, sailing instructor Steve Colgate teaches a crew the fine points of chartering.

the skills necessary for future bareboat charters. At some schools, a seven-day cruise may end with an overnight solo trip without the skipper aboard, although he may follow along in another boat.

Sailing schools are an excellent way for people with small boat experience to upgrade their skills in larger cruising boats. Most schools offer a diploma or certificate at the end of the course and, since they are often operated in conjunction with a charter company, that certificate is often accepted as a substitute for sailing experience when planning a bareboat charter with that particular company.

Be forewarned that a certificate does not give you carte blanche, however, and you'll still be expected to demonstrate your skills to the satisfaction of most charter companies before they turn over one of their bareboats to you.

Special Interest Charters

Because a bareboat charter is such a good way to explore an area in depth, it's no surprise that many charter companies have combined sailing with one or more other areas of interest to attract devotees of both.

You may, for example, find a skin diving charter package that includes a flotilla of bareboats as well as a mothership complete with certified dive instructors, air compressors, and all the other necessities of a skin diving expedition.

Educational charters are often found in Europe, combining some sort of intellectual pursuit into a cruise with a guide aboard. In the Greek islands, for example, there are a number of charters available for those with an interest in archaeology. Either a crewed charter or a flotilla with a mothership will sail between sites of interest, and an archaeologist in the group serves as a guide and lecturer on the subject.

For those who prefer unique animal life, the Galápagos Islands are becoming popular as a destination for crewed charters that include a naturalist to explain the unusual creatures found in this Pacific group.

The Sunsail charter company has set certain flotilla cruises in the Mediterranean aside for singles, allowing crews to meet other sailing-minded singles aboard as many as a dozen yachts.

Nearly any subject that you can dream up, from wine tasting to French cooking to fishing to shell collecting to bird watching, was and can be the basis for a charter. In many cases, these are conceived and executed by a charter company, but there's no reason that you can't gather a group of friends with similar interests and put a charter package together on your own.

Head Boats

These are a combination of a bareboat and a crewed charter, often packaged by a bareboat charter company. In essence, you simply reserve a single berth on a charter boat, where you will be joined by others doing the same thing. If you enjoy making new friends, and don't have enough people to put together a charter crew of your own, then this is the way to go.

The Moorings, for example, offers a "Stateroom Vacations" package that puts you aboard a 50-foot yacht with five other guests, and Sunsail has a "Stowaway Holidays" for singles and couples. You'll have a captain to handle the responsibilities, and you'll share a double cabin with one of your shipmates. You'll do the crew work just as on a bareboat, and you'll have a say in where to go and what to do, but without having to get an entire group together.

GETTING THE MOST FROM YOUR CHARTER

If you're an enthusiastic supporter of packaged tours, where the tour operator herds you on and off the bus at each hotel and sight, then you won't be happy on a charter. A successful charter doesn't just happen and, like any vacation, it requires a certain amount of planning and preparation.

The starting point is to be perfectly honest about your level of experience. If you've skippered cruising yachts for years, then you're probably competent to handle a charter anywhere in the world. If your nautical resume is closer to being a novice, you should select both the boat and the cruising waters more carefully, opting for a simple boat and relatively protected locales.

Other chapters will cover the details of choosing a charter company and the

Snorkeling is one of the great pleasures of chartering, since the waters are often gin-clear and filled with brilliant fish. Take your own mask and fins for a good fit.

Every charter trip results in souvenirs and, in this case, a table is covered with shells on the last day of this power charter.

particular yacht, as well as selecting the cruising area, but advance planning will be the key to the success of your trip.

Most experienced charterers derive as much pleasure from the preparation for the trip as they do on the cruise itself. Investigating the charter companies, scouring the guidebooks to decide upon an area, and making lists of provisions and gear are all a part of the charter experience.

Choosing your crew is equally important, and many an otherwise delightful charter has been ruined by a crew that was incompatible. On the other hand, I've had less-than-perfect charters that were saved because the crew laughed rather than argued, and were willing to bend rather than snap. Don't take a chance on chartering with people that you don't know well.

Instead, assemble the crew from people with your own interests, tastes, and enthusiasms. Living in a relatively confined space on a 24-hour basis for a week can bring out the worst, and the best, in anyone. Careful crew selection is a prime consideration.

WHAT TO EXPECT

Like everything in life, a charter is going to be exactly what you make it. I know of people who have gone off to the most exotic locales, sailed through incredible scenery, and returned home bemoaning the high humidity.

On the other hand, I enjoyed a delightful charter in Scotland where wind and rain were the one constant from the minute we boarded the boat. But my memories are of a warm cabin with good friends, an exciting sail to windward with spray flying, watching a squall approach

from atop a ruined castle, and shrugging off my foul-weather gear in front of a pub's roaring fireplace.

I've had mirror-flat calms during charters in Baja California and again in Thailand, and most of my cruises in the Pacific Northwest have had their share of rainfall. Neither calm nor rain has detracted from the pleasures but, instead, added to the memories. Snuggling back into a warm bunk while the rain patters on the hatch overhead is an exquisite toe-wiggling luxury, and swimming in mid-ocean from a becalmed yacht is a unique experience.

If you expect the weather to always be perfect, the food to be gourmet, and the seas to be calm, then you'll always be unhappy whether you're on a charter yacht, a cruise ship, or at a five-star resort.

Those who get the most out of charters are the people who remain flexible, who are willing to change their plans on a whim or with the weather, and to whom getting there is always going to be less important that enjoying the trip.

When packing your duffel bag for a charter cruise, leave your expectations at home. Open your mind and your spirit, enjoy what you can, and take home memories of incredible sunsets, pristine beaches, and afternoon sails on sparkling waters.

The major charter areas feature warm waters that invite you to spend much of your time splashing round.

2

Choosing a Charter Area

Choosing the area for your charter can often be the trickiest part of your adventure, because so many variables come into play. You'll need to review your preferences, your skills, your budget, and your flexibility to make an educated decision on a charter location.

One starting point is to read the many boating magazines, both in the United States and abroad, which are focusing heavily on the growing chartering market. Many experienced charterers build files of magazine clippings on various areas for reference when they start their decision-making process, but there is one caveat that should be mentioned at this point.

Charter advertising is increasing as this segment of the business continues to blossom. For that very reason, you'll see more articles about chartering than ever before, but keep in mind that magazines are supported by advertising dollars and it is often difficult for the editors to bite the hands that feed them.

In more than two decades in the boating magazine business, I can count the fearlessly critical charter stories on the fingers of one hand, while I've also waded through countless stories that fawned over companies, boats, and areas that I wouldn't recommend to an enemy. Take anything you read with a grain of salt.

One strength of the boating magazines, of course, is the sheer magnitude of the charter company advertising, and you should take advantage of the toll-free numbers for many companies to start receiving their brochures and

Avalon, with its landmark Casino, is the most popular destination from the many Southern California marinas.

promotional materials, which you can use to begin narrowing down the areas that interest you.

Your own location is obviously the starting point for deciding where to take a charter vacation. If you live in the Caribbean, then you can probably eliminate that region from your short list. Charter industry statistics suggest that the vast majority of charterers travel more than 1000 miles to reach their destination, a large number will go 3000 miles, and there is a growing segment that is willing (time and airline fares notwithstanding) to travel into another hemisphere for their charters.

CLIMATE

One of your first general decisions will be the climate that you prefer. It must be obvious that not everyone prefers a temperate climate, or there would be a mass migration to Southern California or Florida. Nevertheless, you should make a conscious decision based on your own climate preferences.

If you dislike cold, then you might want to eliminate many of the northern charter cruising areas of Europe and North America which can be brisk even in mid-summer. On the other hand, if the tropics are too steamy, you may want to skip parts of the South Pacific, Asia,

Trunk Bay on St. John in the U.S. Virgin Islands is popular for snorkeling and swimming. *(Courtesy of the U.S. Virgin Islands Division of Tourism.)*

or lower Caribbean. Bear in mind, of course, that not every area remains the same throughout the year, and you can often find a season that is acceptable. For example, the Pacific Northwest is temperate in the summer, cool in the spring and fall, and downright cold during the winter.

TIME OF YEAR

Your sailing vacation may or may not be dictated by a specific vacation schedule, such as during Christmas or Easter holidays, or during times convenient for your own business. But you should narrow in on your charter window early in your planning, so you can avoid wasting time

The desert landscape of Baja California may be stark, but the protected coves are plentiful and the water is bathwater warm.

on areas that are simply unsuitable. If summer is your only getaway time, for example, you can quickly rule out Baja California because the heat and sun can be unbearable. On the other hand, summer is the ideal time to explore the Apostle Islands of Lake Superior.

Appendix 1 outlines the preferred sailing seasons for a number of different areas, but always bear in mind that weather is one variable that is beyond your control.

BOATING EXPERIENCE

Once again, as I've said several times before, you need to be brutally honest about your level of boating expertise. Areas such as the Virgin Islands and the Bahamas are safe for the novice charterer, with generally protected waters, short distances between anchorages, and predictable weather with good forecasts.

But you'll need a far higher level of skill to tackle chartering in the Hebrides Islands off Scotland, where tidal currents swirl around shoals and rocks, the weather can change suddenly, and good harbors are few and far between.

It's not just the wind and water that can make an area more challenging, but a myriad of other things as well. Foreign waters mean unfamiliar charts, foreign languages, and social factors that compound the normal problems faced by a charter crew. Before you set out to sail the coast of Norway or navigate through the shoals of Belize, be sure of your own skills.

WHAT CAN YOU AFFORD?

Nobody likes to talk about money, and too many otherwise lovely charters have been felled by a shortage of money. Once you've set a certain dollar amount that you're comfortable spending on your vacation, you need to make sure that your planned charter stays within that budget while still leaving a safety margin.

The cost of the bareboat charter is your major expense, and that's easily determined from the company advertising materials. Add to that your airfare or other transportation costs to and from the charter company base, and don't forget all the seemingly minor costs that can add up into sizable chunks, such as airport taxes, meals in transit, taxis or buses, and even overweight baggage if you plan to bring extra gear.

Provisioning is the next major expenditure and, depending upon the area, you may prefer that the charter company handle it at a flat rate per day or from a checklist of supplies. Leave slack in the food budget, though, because you'll surely want to dine ashore.

Besides, even in the most remote areas, I've never been on a charter where we didn't buy food to augment our provisions as we went along. In Baja California, we couldn't resist the lobster and jumbo shrimp offered by the local fishermen. In Tahiti, a few bottles of red wine always seemed to be in the dinghy after forays ashore. In the Mediterranean, every little village had a bakery with mouthwatering pastries that became absolutely necessary to top off the next meal.

Finally, ask the charter company for a list of other specific expenses that their customers encounter, which might include fishing licenses, fuel for the dinghy, mooring fees, harbor fees, document fees (if you cross international boundaries), or any of the other "nickel-and-dime" costs that can break your carefully set budget. One surprise for many crews is a value added tax applied to charters in British or French waters. The French tax (TVA) is 7.5% of the charter cost, figured on a daily basis for each day spent in French waters, and can obviously add several hundred dollars to your budget.

You should also check on fuel, cooking gas, and water. Some companies include these items in the package cost, while others provide you with full tanks at the start of your cruise and then charge you to top them off at the end. In some areas, fuel can be quite expensive and water nearly as precious, so you should understand the policy of your company.

No matter how badly you want to do a particular charter, if it is close to exceeding your budget, you should probably forget it and find a less expensive charter that won't leave you worrying constantly about money.

OTHER CONSIDERATIONS

Obviously climate, time of year, experience and budget are the keys to choosing a charter location, but don't overlook other likes or dislikes that should be taken into consideration.

If your idea of a pleasant vacation is to have dinner at a different restaurant every night, then you should pick an area (such as the Mediterranean) where you can do exactly that. By the same token, if you want to get away from the bright lights and don't care if you see anyone for days on end, then you should pick your charter region accordingly.

Are you a fisherman? Find out what fish are biting and when before you sign up for a fishing-oriented charter.

Do you speak a foreign language and want to air it out? While English is the common language on any waterfront, the locals are delighted to help you with your stumbling efforts to converse and you will find a charter in a country speaking your language to be fun as well as practical for clearing out the cobwebs from your second language.

Picture your prospective charter vacation in your mind: Do you see yourself in solitude or do you want nightlife? Does your spouse rebel at the idea of cooking and want to be served? Do you prefer empty harbors or do you like meeting people in busier anchorages?

3

Choosing a Charter Company

Just as important as picking the right area for your needs is choosing the right charter company. Without putting too fine a point on it, the boating business has always attracted large numbers of dreamers and schemers, and the charter business is no different.

Like the very best waiters, a good charter company is nearly invisible, making sure that everything goes smoothly but without fuss. They pick you up at the airport and ferry you directly to your boat, where you find that all your provisions are ready, the boat is clean and inspected, and your departure briefing is comprehensive but understandable. When you return, the boat is checked in quickly and you are soon on your way home.

A bad charter company (and make no mistake, there are some) can turn the best planned vacation into a frustrating and costly disaster. Even seemingly unimportant things can make a major difference. On one Bahamas charter, we noticed a distinct odor to our boat that we couldn't quite place. It wasn't until one of our crew became ill that we discovered that, for some inexplicable reason, the charter company had decided to spray paint our auxiliary engine the morning of our charter. Our sick crewman was deathly allergic to paint fumes, which reappeared every time we ran the engine.

On a Caribbean charter, with a company specializing in top quality racer-cruisers, we arrived late one night

A fleet of charter yachts awaits new crews at a base on the Caribbean island of St. Martin.

to find that our van driver didn't know where our boat was, nor could he find any of the staff who did and we didn't know the name of our boat, which was somewhere right in front of us. After flying for endless hours, we stood around in the heat and finally someone arrived who found our assigned boat. The following day, the company discovered during our check-out that the anchor windlass didn't work, and we weren't about to hoist the all-chain anchor rode by hand on our luxury charter. The end result was that they couldn't repair the windlass until the next day, so we lost one charter day besides chafing in frustration with nothing to do. Do you think we'd recommend that company? Not likely.

There are more than a few horror stories about bankrupt charter companies disappearing with everyone's deposits, or crooked companies that schedule you for a particular boat and then, upon arrival, claim that boat is broken down and insist that you take a smaller or less acceptable boat instead.

With some amusement, I've read articles in various magazines that suggest a prospective charterer should ask for a bank reference or a Dun & Bradstreet rating, but that seems foolish to me. First, any reputable banker is hardly going to tell a casual caller that Charter Company X is about to go bankrupt, even if he is only too aware that they have less than $100 in their account. At the same time, the number of major companies in all walks of business with good D&B ratings that have fallen to recessionary woes makes me cautious when putting too much faith in such a rating.

While your friends and acquaintances can't put your mind to rest about the financial stability of a charter company, they are certainly a group that you should poll when considering various companies. The boating world is surprisingly small, so it's not unusual for a friend to pass you along to someone you don't know, but who has information of interest.

But most bad charters are the result of small things going wrong, such as a windlass that can't be repaired until the following day, a refrigerator that fails far from the nearest market, or simply worn-out equipment that is obviously patched together.

The large charter companies have most likely grown that way by making sure that their customers went away happy enough to tell others about the experience. Small companies sometimes remain small for just the opposite reasons. Lest this sound like an indictment on a basis of size alone, I should point out that I have chartered quite happily with small charter companies where the personalized service is superb. But, until you have a wealth of experience under your belt, my advice is to stick to the larger fleets.

Large charter companies, like the big car rental companies, have several advantages. First, they usually standardize their fleet to certain types of boats and, in some cases, may even have the yachts built to their own specifications. That makes maintenance easier for the shore crews, and it allows the stockpiling of spare parts for emergencies. In addition, a company with similar boats can quickly substitute an identical replacement in case the yacht you chartered is out of service.

Second, large companies have the ability to send out service boats in case you have problems during the cruise, which would be beyond the scope of a small Mom and Pop operation. Penmar Marine in the Pacific Northwest, for example, not only has a service staff on duty 24 hours a day with a chase boat, but they also maintain a four-place aircraft to fly spares quickly to charter boats in more distant areas.

The Moorings, which has grown into a worldwide charter organization with 25 bases and more than 600 yachts worldwide, has booked more than 200,000 charters, giving it a level of experience unequaled by any of the smaller companies. This enables them to offer the *Four Hour Guarantee,* which gives you either an extra day of charter or a credit for a future free day if any mechanical problem holds you up for four hours.

But where do you start when looking for a charter company? The best place is with the major boating magazines, such as *SAIL, Cruising World* and *Sailing* in the United States, or *Yachting World* and *Yachting Monthly* in England.

In addition to the monthly advertising pages for charter companies, these magazines also produce special sections on chartering in their fall issues (August

A fleet of charter sailboats awaits amid lush foliage in Anse Marcel on St. Martin in the Caribbean.

is often popular) which have editorial material on various charters and comprehensive directories of charter companies by area.

Charter brokers (which you'll find advertising in the above magazines) are in a unique position, since they often represent a multitude of charter companies worldwide. The broker's fees are paid by the charter company, not the client, so your costs will remain the same. Every reputable broker takes the time to visit the various charter sites and actually examine the boats, so you can get good advice on which boats and locations might best suit your needs.

Talk to several charter brokers and see if you develop a rapport. Find out if they have personal knowledge of the boats they represent, and if they have chartered in the areas in which you have an interest. Just as you will with the charter companies, ask for recent references from your broker, preferably for similar boats in your chosen location.

It won't be long before you have a stack of brochures and folders from the charter companies (and you'll continue getting them for years to come, too!). Use these just as a stockbroker uses an annual report to determine the strength of a company but, like a stockbroker, don't forget that numbers can be juggled, so this is just the starting point in your detective work.

With any service oriented business such as chartering, length in business is generally synonymous with quality of service: the good companies survive while the bad ones fail. Unfortunately, the bad ones don't always fail quickly enough.

If you aren't sure how long a company has been in business, go through back issues of boating magazines at the library and see if they have been advertising for several years. Although it creates a Catch-22 situation for new companies, I think five years is a minimum time in business, at least while you're learning the ropes of chartering. After you have more chartering experience, you'll be more capable of making your own decisions as new companies spring into operation.

In reading the literature and the magazine charter directories, you'll soon see how many boats are in the fleet of each company. As I mentioned before, my feeling is that more is better, and I'm wary of any company with less than eight boats. There are exceptions, of course, particularly in exotic locations that may not be able to support more than a few charter boats, or in the case of a resort hotel with a small but well-maintained fleet.

Keep in mind that many companies have several locations, so I feel that a 30-boat fleet at five widely-spaced bases still falls in the small-company category. They can't easily substitute boats, they probably don't maintain full stocks of spare parts at each base, and the number of service personnel is reduced at each location as well.

Ask about the cruising limits for each charter base. The charter company is likely to set out specific boundaries as the outer limits of your charter, perhaps because of international borders or because of hazards. If you have a specific destination in mind, be sure to ask if it is included in their cruising area. Most Virgin Islands charter companies, for example, specifically exclude the island of Anegada for their customers because of its distance from the island chain as well as the underwater hazards surrounding it.

Another factor to check is the vintage of the boats. A charter boat, no matter how well maintained, is subjected to heavy usage and fiberglass boats, regardless of what manufacturers claim, will simply wear out. For years, The Moorings retired every boat after three years of charter service, which is when they had determined that their boats were starting to show their age. Recently, however, The Moorings has added a separate class of charters called the Club Line, which uses slightly older yachts moved from their regular service. Since many of the previously retired yachts from The Moorings wound up as the basis for other charter fleets, the Club Line yachts are aimed at economy-minded charterers who might otherwise have gone to these smaller companies. In this way, a charterer gets a reduced rate without having to give up the service and reliability of a larger company.

Some charter companies buy up the older boats that have been dropped from service with the large charter fleets, and you'll find them advertised using the name given by the original company, such as the CSY 51. Once again, these are older boats that you should consider with extra caution.

Maintenance is a prime factor, since even the best boats need to be carefully serviced. In the large fleets, a boat may charter 35 or more weeks a year, which is a grueling regimen for even the finest construction. Ask about the maintenance procedures, which gives you some insight into what you can expect.

At a very minimum, there should be a 24-hour turnaround time between charters, which allows for cleaning and repair of any minor problems. Stay away from charter companies whose boats come in at ten and go out again at 3 pm.

At The Moorings, for example, each boat is regularly taken out of service, during which time it receives major maintenance, ranging from an engine tune-up to the complete disassembly of anchor and sheet winches. All necessary parts are replaced and, as with most major companies, certain parts and systems are automatically replaced. If their records show that some starter motors begin to fail after 250 hours of service, then the company will replace every starter motor at 200 hours to assure trouble-free cruising.

Be sure to ask about the break-down policy of the charter company. For example, can you call the company collect or do they monitor VHF on a daily basis? If not, you'll be stuck making expensive phone calls to get things fixed. Find out how repairs are handled, too, since some companies may have their own service boats, while others may ask you to have the repairs done by outside contractors.

While you're examining the boats, keep in mind that some charter areas have predominately company-owned boats, while others areas are under a lease-back or management relationship. In the Caribbean, for example, the larger companies either own the boats outright, or have them on such a tight management program that the owner has literally no right to the boat unless he makes a reservation. In the Pacific Northwest, on the other hand, the charter companies rely on a more flexible management role, allowing the owner to do his own maintenance, keep the boat at his own dock, and use the boat whenever it isn't booked for a charter. For just that reason, don't expect to see a look-alike fleet neatly lined up in the Pacific Northwest.

Departure and Arrival Times

Each company sets strict hours for the departure and arrival of their boats, which are geared to allow them sufficient time for cleaning, repairing and restocking each boat before the next crew arrives. In some cases, these departure times can effectively cut a day off your cruising time. One company, for example, sets noon as the end of the charter, but they include the post-cruise check-in as part of your cruising time. While they make every effort to minimize the time it takes to complete the return procedure and inventory (including sending a staff member out to greet you offshore and start the process), the check-in time still counts as part of your cruise. If you arrive only a few minutes before noon, you may be charged extra since your inspection will extend past your return time.

The result is that you are forced to spend your last night within a short distance of the charter base so you can return the boat early in the morning. By the same token, some companies will not release the boat until late afternoon, which almost forces you to stay aboard the first night at their base unless there is enough daylight left to get to a nearby anchorage. Keep both the departure and arrival times in mind as you plan your cruise itinerary. Check your contract, which should stipulate the penalties for late return, regardless of whether it is one hour or six hours.

Sailing Schools

Sailing schools have also entered the charter market in recent years, usually as a sideline to instruction. From stories I've heard, this can be both good news and bad. Obviously, the sailing school is in the business of selling instruction, and some prospective charterers felt they were being strong-armed to take some classes before being allowed to charter the boats.

If you do need instruction, however, this might be the best choice, because the company will know your skills and be more likely to charter a boat to you after you take their course. Your best bet is an organized sailing school, rather than a course offered by a resort as part of their package. Be sure to get a detailed description of the course, and have a clear understanding of how much classroom work is involved, how many days and nights are spent on board, and what type of boat is used.

Ask about the instructors (who should have Coast Guard licenses in the U.S.) and find out about their resumes and sailing background. Last, see how many students are included in the class, and decide whether that is a comfortable number for the intended boat.

As a minimum, a cruising course should include boat handling, anchoring, docking, and navigation.

Networking

Because all charterers face the same fears about charter companies and charter areas, a rather remarkable underground information service has sprung up. Someone in your yacht club knows someone at another club who chartered with the company in question, and is usually more than happy to discuss all the pros and cons at length. To tap into this information source, you need to start asking questions. Don't limit your investigation to friends, but feel free to drop the question at the local marine hardware store, at a nearby sailmaker, or even place a cold call to the commodores of yacht clubs in your area. You'll be surprised by the amount of assistance you get.

There was a wonderful Bob Newhart comedy routine a number of years ago that revolved around a decrepit airline company called the *Grace L. Ferguson Airline and Storm Door Company*, which is quite similar to some charter companies today. Your best bet for a bareboat charter is with a company that does nothing but charters. You may find yacht brokers who also run a small charter fleet out of their marina, usually with boats that are for sale, but these are often ill-maintained because their primary business is selling boats, not vacations.

Remember that Avis and Hertz don't run driving schools, they just lease cars. The fewer things your charter company is trying to do, the more they can concentrate on you as a charterer. Stay as far away from the boatyard-brokerage-charter companies as you would the Ferguson Airline and Storm Door Company.

As you review the literature from the various companies, you might want to make a chart that compares the boats, features and prices. The charter business is extremely price competitive and most companies are within a few dollars of each other, but you'll occasionally find one that is either much more or much less expensive. In either case, it's worth your trouble to find out why.

A more expensive charter may be the result of the company including equipment with their basic charter fee that other companies list as optional, such as an outboard for the dinghy, a spinnaker, or a windsurfer. A less expensive charter may reflect similar shortages which are then balanced when you compare identically equipped boats. Don't be afraid to ask the company about the reason for the difference in price, however. They may be offering a special discount for a particular season or boat, and any reputable company should be able to defend a higher price as well.

Last but just as important as any other item in selecting a company is asking for a list of references. Again, reputable companies have nothing to hide and can usually supply you with names and phone numbers. You should get at least three recent references (within a month), and you should ask specifically for other charterers from your area. That not only minimizes your telephone costs, but it also provides some assurance that you probably aren't calling the parents of the charter company owner.

As I mentioned before, there is an unwritten code among charterers that virtually guarantees you of honest and detailed answers to your questions. Be sure you call all the references with a list of questions in front of you.

4

Selecting a Boat

Selecting a charter boat is an inexact science at best, since it relies so heavily on personal preferences and abilities. While I'm not anti-social, my basic tenets are that bigger boats are better than small boats, and fewer crew is better than many. With that in mind, take the following recommendations with a grain of salt.

First, however, it might be useful to look at the charter market and see how it has evolved, which provides some insight into the choices you'll be facing.

Until the mid-1960s, charters might better have been termed rentals, because the boats were essentially privately owned boats that were simply rented out for a week at a time. But those new-fangled materials of fiberglass, Dacron and aluminum have revolutionized the business so that you can now arrive at a charter base and see 100 absolutely identical sailboats.

The first of the modern large charter companies began when New Jersey dentist John Van Ost came up with the fleet concept, and gathered a group of other professionals to launch Caribbean Sailing Yachts (CSY). They started with a handful of 30-footers that they placed in the British Virgins in 1967 and, as the business blossomed and the concept was accepted, CSY commissioned the Carib 41, a center-cockpit two-cabin yacht that was a novelty in American waters. Instead of owning them outright, as CSY did with their first boats, they sold the boats to individual owners who then turned them over to CSY on a lease-back arrangement that provided each owner

The bow of this Swan 46 is a pleasant place to spend an afternoon, enjoying the sun and spray.

with a fixed monthly payment without any responsibility for upkeep, mooring fees, or insurance. The arrangement also gave CSY complete control over the boats, so they were able to provide a high level of maintenance and reliability.

The Moorings, founded two years later by Charlie and Ginny Cary, started in a similar fashion with a six-boat fleet of Pearson 35s and is now the largest charter company in the world, with hundreds of yachts at more than two dozen bases worldwide. The company has expanded into hotels and resorts, crewed yacht charters, sailing and scuba diving schools, and a comprehensive owner/management program for the yachts which are now built to Moorings specifications.

Jumping into the fray are numerous European-based companies, such as Stardust and Sunsail, which learned the trade in the Mediterranean and have now also established bases worldwide.

As the charter fleets were initially established, the boats were essentially production fiberglass sailboats from U.S. companies such as Morgan and Gulfstar. Because of the decline of the American sailboat business, most of the new charter yachts are coming from European companies such as Beneteau and Jeanneau.

Spinnakers are not part of the usual charter package, but some companies offer them to experienced skippers.

The early boats were often less than stellar performers, and many of them could barely slog to windward at all, relying on their auxiliary engines when the wind was in an unfavorable direction. These boats were also Spartan inside, with vinyl bunk cushions, a smattering of pots and utensils, and cubbyhole head compartments.

Today, however, a modern yacht is not only fully equipped, but luxuriously outfitted. Using an inverter to convert DC power into household current, some yachts feature microwave ovens, blenders and food processors, electric toasters, TVs and VCRs (with a video tape library), compact disc stereos, and even hair dryers. It's not exactly man against the elements and, in fact, it may be what you're trying to escape on your cruise, but there's no escaping the pleasures of a slushy daiquiri in the cockpit after an afternoon sail.

It's not just the luxury that has been improved in modern charter yachts, but the performance as well. Older boats were heavy, beamy, and carried too little sail to make them even marginally exciting, while modern designs are light, lean, and fully rigged for lively sailing. Cruising spinnakers are often an optional accessory and, if you want performance during your charter, be sure to inquire when booking.

Spinnaker flying is a popular pastime in warm climates, using the nylon sail to allow the charter crew to float effortlessly high above the water.

GENERAL CONSIDERATIONS

Two factors tend to govern the choice of the boat: number of crew expected and cost. Taking fewer people on a larger boat obviously increases the cost per person but, in my mind, not enough to discourage the idea. I'd rather spend a few dollars more to ensure a level of luxury than spend an already expensive week wishing I had a larger boat.

Ability is another factor that needs to be taken into account, since you must be able to handle your boat in all conditions, including anchoring, docking, and sailing in strong winds. Four people can handle the modern 50-foot charter yacht easily, but it would be too large for a couple alone, who would be better off with a 40-footer.

I've also found that it's a good idea to leave one bunk free. There always seems to be an overflow of gear that needs a place to be stored, and an extra bunk is a good place for it. This also leaves a little flexibility in the sleeping arrangements, so someone can move if they prefer another bunk.

SIZE

The size of the charter boat is a starting point, although different layouts can make a 35-footer seem like a 40-footer or, unfortunately, vice versa. The charter

A Moorings 50 thunders along, showing that well-designed modern charter boats are fast and powerful.

The hinged table on this yacht folds out of the way so the settee can be used as a lounge as well as a dining area.

company literature will suggest a suitable number of people for each boat although, once again, you need to take this with a grain of salt. The best bet is to study the accommodation plans for each boat, count the number of berths and cabins, and see if this layout seems reasonable for your crew. If you plan to take three couples but the boat has two staterooms with double berths and two single bunks in the main cabin, one couple is never going to be happy about the arrangements.

As I mentioned earlier, I'm a firm believer in having a larger boat, which gives you the space to spread out as well as the maximum level of privacy for everyone. There is, of course, a point of diminishing returns when the boat gets too big to handle easily. By the same token, I prefer to take fewer people than the boat will handle, again to have a resort level of privacy rather than a summer camp with people bunking everywhere.

In many cases, you'll see that there is a forward and an aft cabin, each with a double berth and usually with a private head and shower for each cabin. There may also be a dinette table that converts into a double berth in the main salon, but my recommendation would be to keep that purely for dining and entertaining.

I sailed aboard a charter recently where one extra person was sleeping on that dinette/berth. In the evening, there was always a bit of crashing about as the berth was transformed and, in the morning, the reverse process had to take place before breakfast. Because the main saloon was being used as a bedroom, the rest of the crew had to retire whenever the odd man wanted to sleep, and we had to tiptoe around in the morning until he awoke. It made a 40-foot boat seem cramped.

There is also a rather unique difference between American and European charter sensibilities that I discovered recently during a sail in French Polynesia. Our crew encountered a French group aboard a 32-footer that had four berths in two cabins and a single head. Seven people were aboard the boat! At night they were sleeping on deck and, if it rained, they were stacked like firewood on the cabin floor, yet they were having a marvelous time.

Modern charter yachts are aimed at comfort, such as this one with a permanent dining table in the cockpit and twin steering wheels. The transom swim platform has a folding swim ladder, freshwater shower, and storage lockers for snorkel gear.

As you peruse European charter brochures, remember that there is more of a "bunkhouse" mentality overseas and an attitude that if there is room to sit down, then there must be room to sleep. North Americans prefer more elbow room, and I think that six people need a minimum of two heads, two showers and, preferably, three private staterooms.

LAYOUT

The charter brochures will provide you with drawings of the layout as well as photographs of the interior, and a little eyeballing will give you a good idea of the boat interior.

In many charter fleets, you may have to make a decision between an aft cockpit and a center cockpit layout. The aft cockpit, of course, is where the steering is done from near the stern, with a cockpit located well aft on the boat. A center cockpit, on the other hand, is usually raised above the cabin, placing the steering nearly amidships. Both layouts have their advantages and disadvantages.

Since the center cockpit is located farther forward, it stands to reason that it is closer to any spray coming over the bow and therefore is likely to be wetter. On the other hand, a center cockpit allows for a private and spacious aft cabin behind the cockpit, and generally offers more

The luxurious aft cabin on this charter yacht has a queen-sized berth, settee, and ample storage.

interior room than an aft cockpit yacht of similar size.

An aft cockpit is somewhat drier, plus you don't have as much climbing up and down to get in and out of the cockpit. An aft cockpit yacht tends to have better performance, if only because of less windage but usually because of other compromises that the designers have made in favor of cruising comfort in a center cockpit yacht.

PRIVACY

Yachts are obviously not built like homes, so take into account whatever level of privacy you have in mind. If two staterooms are next to each other with no intervening lockers or heads, then you should assume that the sounds in one cabin will probably be clearly audible in the other. For this particular reason, I like the layouts that put a stateroom at each end of the yacht and use the main saloon, galley and heads as a sound buffer in the middle.

This may seem a minor point, or it may draw snickers from those who picture the sounds of whoopee echoing through the boat, but it can become a point of real irritation on a week-long cruise. After all, how many of you have spent the night separated by only a piece of thin plywood from an adjoining cabin with someone who is even a moderate snorer? And do you really know if your prospective crew snores?

Catamarans are better when it comes to privacy, since the cabins are usually located in each corner of the yacht with ample space between them.

VENTILATION

It's difficult to tell from the brochures whether a boat is claustrophobic inside, or even if it has enough ventilation to be habitable on muggy evenings. You might want to start making notes on various boats of interest, so you can check them out at a local boatshow or even at a dealership. But keep in mind that many of these interiors are changed, often in major ways, for the charter companies.

Aside from the number of berths and heads, I think ventilation is the most important factor in a good charter yacht. Not only must there be a good crossflow of breeze, but it has to be usable in all conditions. Aboard a Beneteau 51 recently, I found it almost impossible to sleep because of the heat belowdecks when we weren't able to open all of the hatches in the torrential rains at night.

I also spent a grim night in the Bahamas many years ago. It was steamy down below but I rigged a windscoop for the hatch over my head and was rewarded with a cool flow of air—until it started to rain and my windscoop became a waterfall. Frantically, I dismantled the funnel and, of course, the rain promptly stopped. For the next hour, I struggled with the same up-down Laurel and Hardy routine until I gave up and fell into an exhausted (and damp) sleep.

One way to check the ventilation is to simply count the number of opening portholes, hatches and vents seen in the brochure photos. As must be obvious, the more the better.

Ask about windscoops, too. There should be a windscoop for every cabin.

WATER

Another precious commodity aboard a charter yacht is water, because you and your crew will probably not use it sparingly. This is, after all, a vacation and not a forced march. In many charter areas, water is also an expensive commodity, and you can find yourself paying a dollar a gallon or more to replenish your tanks. Two showers, plus an on-deck rinsing nozzle for swimmers, can quickly drain the tanks on an average yacht, so make sure there is enough to go around. By the same token, having a saltwater faucet in the galley can ease the onboard drought if you use it to wash dishes, following up with a freshwater rinse.

As a guideline, Sea Recovery, a company that makes reverse osmosis watermakers, suggests that 10 gallons per day per person is sufficient on yachts under 50 feet for showering and domestic chores. A naval architect noted for cruising designs reckons that an economical shower takes about two gallons, washing up in the galley takes another two gallons, and things like shaving, brushing teeth and washing hands takes another gallon, for a minimum of five gallons per person per day. For comparison's sake, then, a four person crew needs between 20 and 40 gallons per day and a six person crew needs 30 to 60 gallons per day.

Using those numbers, it's interesting to check the water capacity on various boats, and you'll find some wide variations. It's obvious you'll need to conserve water, but choose your boats carefully as some are more critical than others.

SAILING GEAR

Nearly every modern charter yacht relies on roller-furling headsails to simplify sail handling and, while they're not the latest in racing sails, they will greatly simplify your charter. Some charter yachts are now using various types of furling mainsails and, in my opinion, any type of workable sail handling system that reduces the effort or manpower required is a boon on a charter.

Many charter yachts now have systems that virtually eliminate having to furl the mainsail. Simply release the halyard and the mainsail drops snugly into a canvas "nest" that keeps it tidy and ready for immediate use.

ANCHOR GEAR

An electric anchor windlass is one of the luxuries that is often overlooked until you have to up-anchor in deep water, and then it goes near the top of the checklist for every sailor looking at potential charters.

The length of the anchor rode and the amount of chain will be different for varying areas. In the South Pacific, all chain anchor rodes are normal, since they offer protection from chafe on the coral reefs. In other parts of the world, however, you may be using a combination of chain and line. Your boat should have at least one stern anchor or spare along with sufficient rode to moor the yacht if something happens to your bow anchor.

GALLEY

The galley must be large enough to handle the dining needs of the entire crew, as well as any guests you may invite aboard. If you're feeding a large crew, you might want to make sure the galley is large enough for two people, so you can invite a helper to share the work.

The refrigerator/freezer should have sufficient capacity to store a week's worth of goodies, although some charter companies can provide additional ice chests for any over-supply. Most charter yachts have mechanical refrigeration systems driven by the engine, but there are still a few of the smaller boats that rely on blocks of ice. Find out what to expect ahead of time, because ice can be a problem in a tropical climate.

EQUIPMENT

The equipment list for each yacht is a major variable, and each company approaches the gear question differently. Some assume that you can pick the items you want from a list of extras, while others simplify their operation by putting everything on board.

This center-cockpit Swan charter yacht has a bimini top to shade the cockpit while under sail.

In every case, a good bimini top is a starting point for any sunny climate, and you should look at the photos of the yachts in the brochures, as you'll see some wide variation in the size of these tops. In one photo, for example, it was clearly evident that the bimini covered only about half of the cockpit, leaving the helm area completely unprotected as well as the forward end of the cockpit. That means that the helmsperson will always be in the sun, and you won't be able to stretch out in the cockpit with your back against the cabin, either. The bimini should also be usable when under sail, and not just when powering or anchored.

The charter area also imposes some variables on the standard equipment. Sunsail, for example, provides outboard motors as standard equipment for the dinghy in the Caribbean, but not in the Mediterranean where more time is spent in marinas than at anchor. Rigid dinghies are supplied in the Caribbean (to withstand the constant beaching on rock and coral), while inflatables are used in the Mediterranean to conserve space since they aren't used as often.

Cockpit cushions are another nicety that can make a great difference in the crew comfort. You'll be sitting in the cockpit while sailing, and sitting in the cockpit at anchor, so you'd better be comfortable. On the standard equipment list of some charter companies, such as Sunsail, they list "teak seating or cockpit cushions" as though they were the

same, but I'll take the padding anytime. Ask before you go.

The only entertainment aboard charter boats in the past was whatever local radio station you could find on the direction-finder but, today, you're likely to find a complete radio and stereo system as a minimum, and many yachts have televisions, cassette and CD players, and video libraries. Bring your own tapes or CDs of favorite sounds, because you can't rely on the selection found on board.

This yacht has a bimini top to shade the skipper but not the crew. Storing the outboard on the stern bracket is safer than leaving it on the dinghy while towing.

5

Catamarans

It should come as no surprise, especially if you've been looking at charter ads, that the catamaran is a growing force in the charter world. In just a few years, multihulls have evolved from being just "beach cats" to sleek and luxurious fiberglass cruising yachts in great demand among the charter fleets.

Relatively new in Caribbean and Pacific charter fleets are the catamarans that have been accepted with such fanfare in Europe. Pun aside, catamarans really are a different breed of cat from conventional sailboats.

In general, a catamaran is somewhat faster but far roomier than a similarly sized monohulled sailboat. A 48-foot catamaran, for example, will have four large staterooms (one forward and one aft in each hull) that are well separated for privacy, as well as a spacious saloon and galley in the deckhouse spanning

These two 82-foot catamarans provide exceptional speed and luxury for Caribbean charters.

Catamarans such as this Privilege 48 offer extensive deck space, and can comfortably accommodate more people than monohulls of the same length.

the two hulls. The saloon may have comfortable seating for a dozen or more people, while the cockpit may seat two dozen more easily. Many catamarans have twin steering wheels so the helmsperson has a good view from either side of the boat, and twin engines are the normal power.

Knifing through the water creates less spray, and the big net trampolines between the two bows are a wonderful place to sprawl and watch the water flash past. On one catamaran charter, we had a school of dolphins play just inches away from us.

A second feature of the catamaran is stability, since the widely spaced hulls counteract the leverage of the sails. Most catamarans rarely heel more than 5 degrees in normal conditions, so it is a good boat for anyone worried about tipping over.

Another feature is the shallow draft, which allows some catamarans to anchor in water shallow enough to walk ashore, although you always need to be careful of rudders and propellers.

Catamarans take getting used to, since they react slowly to the rudder, and they have large turning radii compared to monohulls, but anyone with experience in a similar size sailboat can quickly adapt to catamaran sailing.

Many skippers with monohull experience view cats with a mixture of alarm

One advantage of catamarans is the immense deck space, which is ideal for sunning or just sprawling with a good book.

and caution, since catamarans have a reputation for being difficult to maneuver (particularly when tacking) and the small beach cats seem to capsize on a whim, which isn't reassuring when you're skippering an eight-ton 43-foot catamaran in a growing breeze.

Many of the differences, however, are only in the mind of the monohull sailor and, as one experienced catamaran charterer pointed out, "a catamaran is just like a monohull that happens to be 22-foot wide."

There are three specific areas that the charter companies focus upon when showing a monohull sailor how to handle a charter cat: sailing, powering, and anchoring.

SAILING

While fully-battened mains are now found on many monohulls, the concept is still unfamiliar to many sailors, which results in a low level of performance because they simply don't know how to trim a fully-battened mainsail. Because there is little or no "luff bubble" to give a visual indication of sail trim, most newcomers to catamarans overtrim the main and the resulting lack of speed is a frequent cause of complaint to the charter fleet operators.

To get the best performance from a fully-battened main, particularly on a wide-beamed boat like a catamaran, you need to rely completely on the telltales on the mainsail. Make sure that you're getting a good laminar air flow on both sides of the sail, and be wary of strapping the boom (and the leech of the sail) too tightly. The mainsail is the most powerful sail on most charter catamarans, and skippers should pay more attention to it than to the genoa.

Tacking is another point of concern for monohull skippers, who are used to simply turning the wheel and changing tacks. Because the twin hulls resist turning, a catamaran does take considerably more finesse to tack, but you won't have any problems if you remember a few pointers.

First, time your tack to have as much speed as possible when you turn the wheel. This means watching for larger than usual seas that might stall the boat, as well as being careful not to pinch up too close to the wind beforehand with a resultant loss of speed. As you tack, be sure to release the mainsheet traveller several feet, which will help to keep the boat from weather-cocking (where the boat acts like a windvane) into the wind and stopping. If you are sailing in light winds or steep seas, you can backwind the jib to push the bow around. Once on the new tack, trim in the mainsheet traveller and look aloft to make sure that all the battens have popped over onto the new tack.

This crewed catamaran anchored off Huahine in French Polynesia usually carries a skipper and a single crew who doubles as chef and hostess.

The sailing angles for a modern cat are essentially those of a monohull but, in some sea conditions (short and choppy, for example), footing off will provide more power and speed.

POWERING

Charter catamarans uniformly have an engine in each hull, which gives them the handling characteristics of a twin-engined powerboat. This not only provides you with get-home power if one engine has a problem, but it also makes close-quarters maneuvering a cinch as long as you understand the principles. With widely spaced engines, you can literally rotate a cat in little more than its own length, making it possible to squeak into a tight spot that would be unavailable to a monohull.

One charter check-out skipper compared maneuvering using the twin engines of a catamaran to driving a tracked land vehicle. Simply rest your hands on the shift levers while the engine is at idling speed. Push forward with the lever on the outside of your turn and pull back on the lever on the inside of your turn. For example, to turn a catamaran clockwise, push forward on the port shift and reverse on the starboard. If a tracked vehicle isn't in your transportation repertoire, another check-out skipper suggested thinking of the reins on a horse: pull back on the side toward which you want to turn, while giving slack (pushing forward) on the other side. Either way, it's a technique that you can pick up quickly and use to make yourself look like a real pro while docking.

Catamarans are also quick to accelerate, so be sensitive to using the throttles, particularly when docking. Use small bursts of power to get the boat moving, and you're likely to be surprised at how fast you're going when compared to the relatively slow reaction of a monohull.

A catamaran also has considerable windage and a small keel area, making it more sensitive to wind than a monohull. When docking or maneuvering in strong crosswinds, keep drift in mind so you aren't blown sideways into an awkward situation.

ANCHORING

Catamarans have a reputation for *hunting* at anchor, or literally sailing back and forth at the end of the anchor rode, making for an uncomfortable night. This is almost always a result of where the anchor rode attaches to the catamaran since, on many cats, the anchor roller may be well aft of the actual bows, either on the cross-member between the hulls or on the hull forward of the mast. Either way, the boat will pivot on this point.

The solution is to move the pivot point in front of the boat. Many charter cats are now equipped with removable anchor bridles that are attached to each hull at the very bow. Set your anchor normally, hook the bridle to the anchor chain, and then ease out more rode so that the load is carried entirely by the bridle at a point forward of the hulls. No more hunting.

6

Powerboat Charters

Bare powerboat charters are a new entry into the world of chartering, which was once confined to sailing yachts or larger crewed motoryachts, but many areas now have yachts available for non-sailors.

Surprisingly enough, many of the powerboat charterers are actually sailors, who have decided that the comforts of power cruising are worth giving up the pleasures of sailing.

But, whether you're a sailing expert venturing into new worlds or a novice testing your powerboat skills, you'll need to be prepared for the differences in power charters.

For anyone used to sailing, powerboats have advantages and drawbacks. The first advantage is that they're ready to go at the turn of a key, unlike sailboats where the sails have to be hoisted and adjusted regularly. The second advantage is that powerboats are fast and dry. You'll be able to cruise from harbor to harbor at much higher average speeds than similarly sized sailboats and, from the protection of the fly bridge, you'll miss most of the spray. In rain, you can retreat to the main cabin of many powerboats, where there is a second helm station for just such conditions.

The disadvantages of powerboats, particularly for sailors, are the opposites of the above advantages. Many sailors take pleasure in sailing, and the delights of a sunny afternoon under an expanse of white sail is lost on a powerboat. Even spray—that occasional mist that tingles on warm skin—is part of the sailing lifestyle, and not everyone is willing to give it up.

This charter powerboat has a hardtop over the aft deck that provides a shaded dining area, as well as a bimini top over the flybridge.

CHOOSING A POWERBOAT

In general, you get a great deal more space aboard a powerboat than you do on a similarly sized sailboat, so you need to reset your thinking when preparing to switch from sail to power. While a 45-foot sailboat may be the right size for three couples, a 40-foot powerboat may offer larger staterooms, a bigger galley, and more usable deck space for sunning.

Once again, my own personal preference is that more room for less people is the best choice. Just as with a sailboat, I prefer not to use the main saloon for a bedroom, so that the crew isn't restricted in getting up early or searching for a cold soft drink at midnight. Many of the powerboats used in chartering have the ubiquitous *convertible dinette* found on sailboats, which can be converted from a dining table during the day to a berth at night but, unless you really need the extra bunk, don't count this area as a cabin. There's usually no storage for your personal gear, you have to share a head compartment with one of the other cabins, and you have to put your bedding away by day and make your bed every evening after dinner. That's too much like work for my taste.

When you look at the accommodation plans, you'll probably see a few layouts with a big aft stateroom, a forward stateroom, and a smaller cabin to one side between the two.

A fleet of chartered powerboats anchors close to the beach at Virgin Gorda in the British Virgin Islands. (Courtesy of VIP Yacht Charters)

The "galley-up" arrangement on this powerboat allows the cook to be a part of the saloon conversation, as well as having plenty of light and air.

The aft stateroom is the traditional owner's cabin on most powerboats, so it will usually have a large double or queen-sized berth, a private head compartment with shower, and such amenities as bedside bureaus, a vanity area, and a large hanging locker.

The forward cabin will also have a double berth, although it will probably be more V-shaped to fit the bow, and it will have a smaller head compartment and less storage.

My experience has been that the smallest stateroom is the least desirable, and not just because of size. Sometimes with a double berth but more often with upper and lower bunks, it's considerably smaller and less ventilated than the others, which can be a real drawback in the tropics.

GALLEY UP OR DOWN?

One choice not faced by sailboat charterers is selecting the location of the galley which, in powerboats, can be either *up* or *down.* A galley up configuration means that the galley is on the same level as the main saloon, and is usually located either to one side or in a forward corner out of the way. This layout reduces the size of the saloon, but it puts the cook into the middle of the dinner hour conversation, as well as providing the best view and the maximum amount of light and fresh air.

A galley down layout puts the cooking area at the level of the forward cabins, and provides more space in the saloon for entertaining. The drawback to a galley down is that the cook is separated from the saloon, either by height or by actual divider, and there is usually little or no view from the galley.

POWER

Another choice faced by potential power charterers is the number of engines. Smaller powerboats, such as trawlers in the 35-foot size, often have single engines, while larger yachts usually have twin engines. Everything else being equal, I would opt for twin engines in most cases for several reasons.

First, a second engine is a sizable safety factor, especially when you don't have sails to fall back upon if your single engine fails for any reason. Second, twin-engined powerboats are so much easier to maneuver, particularly in difficult docking situations or with wind and current pushing you around, that even novices can end up looking like pros. Last, twin-engined boats are generally faster than singles and, since speed is one of the advantages of a power charter, you may as well take full advantage of it. The downside to a twin-engined boat, of course, is that it has twice the fuel consumption which, at today's fuel prices, can make a sizable difference in your budget.

Speaking of mechanical systems, another advantage of the powerboat charter is that these yachts usually have generators, which provide an electrical supply for every possible amenity from blenders to air conditioning. Whether you care if your margaritas or daiquiris are blended may of be of little importance, but an air conditioning

This 37-foot sportfisherman had the luxury of air conditioning to counter the hot days in Mexico's Sea of Cortez.

Powerboats often anchor together since the noise of their generators can be irritating, particularly to boats that don't have the benefits of air conditioning and blenders.

system can truly put you into the luxury category. If the weather is hot and humid, being able to dine and sleep in a cool environment can literally be priceless, especially if you don't have it!

But having a generator does require you to be a good neighbor. It's nice to sleep with the air conditioning on all night, but that also requires the generator when you're anchored, and that means a steady exhaust note for the boats around you. If you plan to run your generator all night, find an anchorage away from everyone else so you don't disturb the evening quiet. As an alternative, you may choose to marina-hop in your powerboat, spending each night tied to a pier with a supply of shorepower for your needs.

A vintage trawler-style powerboat is perfect for one couple to handle in the Bahamas.

USING THE POWERBOAT

Since you have an advantage of speed, powerboat charterers are able to leave later and still arrive earlier than sailboats, so you can dally at anchor until late morning and then reach your next destination while the prime anchorages are still available. Or you may leave early and then explore coves or islets along the way, relying on your speed to get in before dark. Whatever your choice, a powerboat widens your horizons to more distant ports, or you can use it for getting the most out of a smaller area.

I chartered a 37-foot powerboat in Baja California several years ago, and it turned out to be one of my most enjoyable charters ever. Although it was a two-cabin layout, there were just two of us aboard, and it made a delightful yacht for a couple. The master stateroom on this sportfishing-styled yacht was forward, with a second cabin with upper and lower bunks next to it, and a shared head with shower. The second cabin was tiny and airless, and we ended up using it to store our overflow of clothes, books and gear.

With twin engines, we had the speed to cruise far from the charter base but, instead, we chose to do a more leisurely exploration and never ventured more than 40 miles from home base. But we did take pleasure in sleeping late and then watching the sailboats up-anchor to set sail for their next harbor. We snorkeled the reefs or explored until after lunch, which was held in the air conditioned saloon. Even with such a late start, we were still among the first to arrive at the next anchorage, often sipping our slushy

This Hatteras sportfisherman lies at anchor in a quiet cove off Phuket in Thailand.

A lone powerboat takes advantage of its shallow draft to anchor near the boulders of Virgin Gorda in the British Virgin Islands. *(Courtesy of VIP Yacht Charters.)*

Anchored near a sandy beach, this power charter crew is enjoying warm Caribbean waters from the swim platform on the stern.

blended daiquiris when the sailboats finally dropped anchor.

Powerboats also have a draft advantage, and can usually anchor in shallower water than sailboats, which are kept to deep water by their keels, which gives you two advantages. First, since shallow water is usually closer to shore, you are in more protected surroundings and will ride easier. Second, because most charter areas have far more sailboats than power, you can usually find a good spot in shallow water even if the deeper water anchorage is crowded with sailboats.

POWERBOAT SEAMANSHIP

Just because you have some advantages over sailboats doesn't mean you can let your guard down, however, and you need to exercise the same cautious seamanship that you would under sail.

Sailboats can usually run aground with impunity, and the worst damage is often just a little scuffed paint on the bottom of the keel. On a powerboat, however, the propellers, prop shafts and rudders are completely exposed and quite vulnerable. If you find a stray coral head with your powerboat, you may also find that you've bent a propeller or a shaft.

Without the benefit of a keel and because of the greater windage from the larger superstructure and topsides, powerboats are more affected by the wind. When docking, you need to take into account the windage, since it can easily push you toward (or away from) a pier.

With a single engine, you'll need to be more confident in your boat handling so, on your first day of the charter, you should practice stopping, reversing, and tight turns just as you would with a sailboat. Most single-engined boats have right-hand turning propellers, which means the propeller turns clockwise when in forward gear and when viewed from the stern looking forward. A right-hand prop pushes the stern to starboard in forward gear, and pulls it to port when reversed. Use this knowledge to help with your boat handling. If possible, approach a dock on your port side and use reverse to both pull the stern into the dock and stop the boat.

Twin-engined powerboats don't have this pull, since the two engines rotate in opposite directions to balance each other out. With both engines in reverse, the boat will back in a straight line. But because the propellers are offset from the centerline, using either engine by itself will cause the boat to turn. For example, putting either engine alone in forward pushes the bow toward the opposite side, i.e. the starboard engine in forward will cause the boat to turn to port.

With twin engines, you'll be able to "twist" the boat within its own length by judicious use of shift and throttle. By putting one engine in forward and the other in reverse, you can turn the boat quickly to either side. Imagine that the shift levers are the rim of a steering wheel or the handlebars of a bicycle. When you push forward (forward gear) on the starboard shift and pull back (reverse gear) on the port, the boat will turn to port. Reverse the procedure, and the boat will spin to starboard.

You'll need to experiment a bit; you may require more throttle on the reversed engine to stay in position, since the propeller is less effective in reverse than when going forward.

In heavy winds, you may find it uncomfortable going directly into the seas, so choosing a course on either side of the wind and then tacking toward your destination will allow the boat to ride comfortably over the waves without free falling at the top.

Going downwind in big seas is easier if you can set your speed to match that of the waves, so you aren't either catching or being caught by the swells. If possible, keep your yacht on the face of the wave so that you're always going downhill with maximum control and minimum effort on the engines.

7

Picking Your Crew

The military spends considerable time and money screening candidates for their submarine and bomber crews, as well as anyone who will be sent to a remote outpost, but most charter crews are gathered up from casual friends at the yacht club bar.

For once, the military minds are right. Put six people on a 40-footer for a week and you have a breeding ground for emotional conflicts. Stir in some bad weather and you can reach the flashpoint quickly.

As I mentioned earlier, I'm a strong believer in fewer crew rather than many, which gives everyone more personal space and relieves the conflicts of waiting to use the head, dining in a crowd, or even finding places to stow gear.

I think personality is the best starting point, and I prefer to sail with people who have a ready sense of humor and a relatively mild temper. Too many little things can (and do) go wrong aboard any boat with great regularity that you have to simply grin and bear it.

As someone who values the quiet times, such as curling up in the cockpit with a good book, I find that a non-stop talker can be an abrasive element. A Chatty Cathy or Talky Tommy can dim the beauty of the most outrageous sunset.

By the same token, personal habits can also make or break a cruise. If you're not a smoker, then descending into a cabin filled with a blue haze will grow old quickly. Even smokers who are considerate enough to smoke only on deck (and to leeward) carry an aroma with them that can set off an avid anti-smoker, and most charter companies that assemble crews for flotillas will allocate certain boats as smoking or non-smoking.

Drinking is another consideration, although there are occasionally startling discoveries found on charter cruises. The mild-mannered friends who sip wine at your home during dinner can turn into sloppy drunks on their vacation time, and it's sometimes hard to ferret out these problems ahead of time.

Common interests doesn't just mean that you all enjoy Ludlum novels (although being able to share books on a cruise is a real asset!), but includes your outlook and expectations. Some friends of mine chartered with another couple and, too late, discovered that the other twosome wanted to go ashore and party every night. There was a constant conflict between dinner aboard or ashore, as well as allocating the use of the dinghy for an entire evening. It also meant that one couple was always pushing to reach the next harbor in time for happy hour ashore, while my friends would have preferred to leisurely explore new coves and anchorages.

The head on this yacht is compact, with storage for toiletries in lockers and drawers.

Skill level can be a factor or not, depending upon the people. I've sailed with crews of absolute novices who were challenged by learning to sail but maintained their humor throughout any crisis. I've also sailed with crews of highly experienced sailors who squabbled constantly about everything from sail trim to anchoring procedure.

As a general rule, I'm a firm believer that there should be at least two experienced sailors aboard every charter, just as a hedge against emergency. Every so often I hear stories of charter boats circling helplessly after the skipper fell overboard, because no one in the crew knew how to start the engine or even radio for help. This may be a moot point, however, since most charter companies share my concern and expect a minimum level of competency from other crewmembers.

By the way, relatives fall into exactly the same category as all other crewmembers, and you should be prepared to include or omit them for all the same reasons. Just because you are related to a person doesn't necessarily mean they will fit into a charter situation and, in some cases, that relationship is a hindrance.

Professional charter boat crews sometimes mention a CFH (Crew From Hell), hopefully not referring to you, but there is also the PC (Perfect Crew), who will have most, if not all, of the following traits on a bareboat charter:

1. They offer to share the cost of fuel and food without being asked.
2. They don't arrive with six pieces of hard-sided Samsonite luggage but, instead, have no more than a large duffel bag.
3. They bring a selection of paperback books which they share with the rest of the crew.
4. They don't understand boredom.
5. They respect quiet time and privacy.
6. They eat what is prepared for them by others.
7. They share the cooking and cleaning chores without being asked.
8. They don't hog the helm and, conversely, offer to help sail the boat.
9. They are tidy, and put away their personal gear, especially when they are sleeping in a common area of the boat.
10. They leave the head compartment cleaner than when they entered.
11. They bring their own suntan potions, snorkel gear and seasickness remedies.
12. They don't hog the dinghy, or take it ashore and strand the crew.
13. They volunteer to help with the hard work, such as raising sail or hoisting the anchor.
14. They take and offer advice gently and calmly.

8

Paperwork

BOOKING THE CHARTER

Once you've made your decision about the boat, the location, and the specific time you want your charter vacation, it's time to make the reservation.

Most companies have a toll-free number for you to call, and the operators will have either the master charter book or the same information on a computer. You'll usually start with the date and the location, followed by the boat type, and they can quickly check on availability for you.

In some cases, they may not have the exact dates you want, and will ask if you can move your arrival or departure dates one way or the other by a few days. The specific boat may also not be available, in which case they can recommend an acceptable substitute.

Each company varies in its policies, but some are willing to negotiate a reduced price on a larger boat if the one that you requested is unavailable, so be sure to ask for a discount if that is the case.

Once you've come to an agreement on the date, location, boat and price, the charter agent will hold your reservation for a set period, usually from 10 to 14 days. During that time, the company will send you an information packet with a written confirmation, which should outline all of the details agreed upon by telephone, along with a sailing experience questionnaire for the skipper and each crewmember to fill out.

An invoice for your deposit will also be in the packet and, again, each company has different policies. Some companies require a 50% deposit to hold the booking. Others ask for only 25% at the time of the reservation, with another 25% due 90 days prior to the charter and the remainder due 30 days beforehand.

The Charter Questionnaire

Every charter company will send you a questionnaire regarding your experience as well as that of other members of the crew. They'll use this to make sure that you're capable of being turned loose in the charter area of your choice. You'll need to return this questionnaire with the other paperwork as you book your charter and, more than anything else, this questionnaire will decide your chartering fate.

In most cases, they will ask about previous charters and specifically about those where you were in command. They'll ask whether you own a boat, its size, and in what areas you normally sail. They'll want to know if you've cruised (or raced) outside your home waters before, and you'll also need to indicate your navigational experience.

Every charter company has stories of skippers whose questionnaires made them sound like America's Cup winners but who, in person, barely knew one end of the boat from another. In some cases, these imposters have been allowed to hire a skipper for the duration of their charter but, in some instances, have simply been refused the charter, losing a portion of their deposit in the process.

A more honest approach by a young couple with basic sailing skills (but no navigational experience) resulted in a positive experience. The charter company, upon reviewing their questionnaire, realized these first-timers were requesting an area that demanded more than their abilities. A company representative called them and tactfully suggested they might have a better time by choosing a less demanding area. They agreed, spent a wonderful week sailing with no problems whatsoever, and have now been chartering twice a year in progressively more challenging areas to build up their skills.

Transportation

In many cases, the charter company will also handle your transportation to and from the charter base and they can often get you a better price on airfares than your own travel agent, simply because they buy blocks of airline seats, secure in the knowledge that they will have boats full of arriving charterers.

I'm a strong believer in arriving at least one day before the charter is due to start, which allows some slack in case of missing luggage and missed or delayed airline flights, not to mention a chance to catch up on jet lag. I don't much fancy setting out in an unfamiliar and expensive yacht through foreign waters, particularly feeling as I do after getting off a 14-hour flight through six time zones.

I also try to book flights that are either open-ended, or allow for me to change my return trip with a minimal fee. This permits me to stay for an extra day if I find something interesting and, if there are boat problems, I can make up the time at the end of my charter rather than being locked in to a departure time.

While many charterers routinely ship their duffel bags, I prefer to put my duffel bag inside a hard-sided suitcase and ship it with protection. I don't want to break anything inside the duffel, and the airlines are notably cavalier about dropping suitcases onto softer luggage. Second, I like the security against theft that a hard suitcase provides. Last, I've seen duffel bags sitting on the runway at small island airports in pouring rainstorms when the ground crew took shelter, and I knew that someone was going to live in wet clothes for a day or two. Most charter companies (check beforehand) have provisions for storing hard luggage during your charter.

A final word about luggage. I would recommend that you check your baggage through to the last major airport in your itinerary, and then hand carry it onto the small commuter airline yourself to make sure that you and your baggage arrive at the same time.

As a photographer, I prefer not to have any of my film x-rayed, so I empty all my film canisters out of their cardboard and plastic containers and put them all together in a clear Ziploc bag that I hand carry through security, and I've never had any problems with officials refusing to inspect them visually.

Cancellations

Make sure that you clearly understand the refund policies in case you cancel. Nearly all companies charge a fee (often $100 or more) for cancellations for any reason before 90 days and, in many cases, will not issue any refunds with less than 90 days before the charter date.

Most of the larger charter companies (as well as your local travel agent) offer a travel insurance package that will reimburse your deposit after a cancellation, but you should carefully check the risks covered. In most cases, they are limited to cancellations caused by circumstances outside your control, such as medical emergencies, civil unrest, airline strikes, etc. Cancelling a charter simply because you decided not to go is usually not grounds for a refund.

Security Deposit

All companies require a refundable security deposit to cover damage or missing gear from the yacht. The amount of this deposit varies depending upon the value of the yacht and the deductible on the insurance coverage, but it usually falls between $500 and $2000. That deposit won't be returned to you immediately after the cruise because the company may take 24 hours to fully check over the boat, which is why I recommend that you pay with a credit card rather than with cash. The credit card not only leaves you with cash for travelling, but it also allows you to dispute any charges at a later date. Nevertheless, be sure that your contract specifies exactly when and how the deposit will be refunded.

Insurance

With many charters, the company provides all risk insurance coverage for major damage or loss of the vessel and simply includes that as part of your charter fee. Bear in mind, however, that you are responsible up to the amount of the deductible for any damage that is your fault. Be sure that you fully understand the amount of the deductible, and make sure the insurance covers the dinghy and other watercraft such as windsurfers. Your contract will also specify the limits of liability and indemnity insurance for you and your crew, so be sure to read and understand all the paperwork.

Minor damage caused by the charterer, such as dropping winch handles overboard, losing an anchor, or dunking the outboard, will be deducted from the security deposit. Most charter companies offer an insurance package to cover these accidents, with a cost of $10-$15 per charter day, but they do not cover gross negligence, so you must always use good seamanship and common sense.

Keep in mind also that the deductible applies to each incident and not to the entire cruise. If you gouge the hull while docking (at a cost of $500), dunk the outboard (another $500), and rip the mainsail by crew error ($2000), you are liable for a total of $1500 even if the deductible is only $500, because there were three separate incidents. My advice is to take the additional insurance, which then frees you from any security deposit and leaves you to enjoy your cruise without worries. You can also just walk away from the boat at the end of the trip without any concerns.

The charter company will absorb the cost of any breakdowns that are not the result of negligence on your part (such as broken refrigeration) and your charter contract should clearly state that routine wear and tear is covered by the company.

Read and remember all the rules set by the charter company, since these can affect your insurance coverage. Every charter company prohibits sailing at night and, if you sustain damage to the boat while underway at night, the insurance company is likely to sue you to recover the costs. In most cases, your cruising area will be specifically outlined, so be careful to remain within the accepted limits. Before you leave, the charter company will probably ask you to sign a separate agreement stating that you understand the limitations on the charter and that you understand the rules for insurance coverage.

Read the fine print in the contract (and insurance policy) carefully, so you fully understand the many exclusions that are probably there. For example, most insurance policies exempt coverage for *gross negligence* or *willful carelessness,* rather broad terms that should keep lawyers happily debating in court for years. When you initially book the charter, you should request a copy of the insurance policy along with the contract and, if you have any questions, consult your own attorney or clarify them with the charter company in writing beforehand.

If you are chartering from a private party, be sure to ask for a copy of their insurance policy and read it carefully to see that it covers bareboat chartering. Few conventional marine insurance policies include chartering coverage, and this must either be added with a separate rider or by a commercial charter policy. Many boat owners try to slide through on this coverage, because charter insurance is considerably more expensive than a normal policy, but such corner-cutting leaves you exposed to a lawsuit. You may have recourse against the boat owner, but you are still liable for damages or injury to a third party.

Other Problems

While bankruptcy is not a common problem in the charter business, it does happen from time to time, and more than a few charterers have lost their deposits in the process. There simply isn't any good solution to this problem, other than asking the charter company to bond your money or place it in an escrow account, which few (if any) will do because they need the money to cover operating costs. If possible, pay with a credit card such as Visa, MasterCard or American Express, because the major card companies will refund charges made on their cards for services not received. They also act as an ombudsman when there is a dispute over charges with the charter company.

Interestingly enough, sometimes the charter industry takes care of its own. When CSY, a large charter operation in the British Virgin Islands, went out of business in early 1992, they had more than 130 booked charters they could not fulfill. In a magnanimous gesture of good will, The Moorings agreed to provide yachts for the stranded sailors, commenting that when small companies fold and leave vacationers high and dry, it hurts the entire industry.

What do you do if your boat is not available when you arrive? This usually occurs only with loosely run management fleets, where the owner may suddenly break his contract with the company or the boat may be damaged beyond immediate repair. Every company has boat problems, ranging from broken masts and engines to actual sinking, but the larger fleets usually have the resources to shuffle a number of boats as substitutes until repairs can be made.

Whatever the situation, your charter contract should clearly bind the company to provide an immediate and suitable replacement, even if it means giving you a larger yacht at the original price. No company is going to refund your travel costs or out-of-pocket expenses, which is why you should investigate travel insurance for your own protection. But, at worst, the charter contract should spell out the full and immediate return of your deposit, or provide for other acceptable arrangements, such as a free charter at another time. But, as any lawyer will tell you, unless you have such a clause in your charter contract, you will have little recourse later.

The Moorings contract guarantees that they will provide you with a comparable yacht if a problem arises that prevents you from sailing. In addition, if you lose more than four hours sailing time on a charter in the Bahamas, Caribbean or South Pacific, they will make it up either in additional sailing time, or monetary credits on future charters.

If you have a particular reason for wanting a specific boat, such as testing it prior to buying a similar model, write to the company ahead of time and request a guarantee in writing. Also check on the policy if the boat is not ready when you arrive. Will the company provide compensation for lost time, and will they pay for your hotel room?

Inventory List

Every charter company will provide you with an inventory list of the equipment on your boat, usually covering everything from the dinghy outboard to the corkscrew in the galley. They'll mention the list during the check-out and you'll probably be asked to initial a copy as well, but, during the rush to get underway on your vacation, it is often forgotten.

Take the time to go over the checklist carefully before you cast off, however, because the charter company uses that same list when you return and you are responsible for any missing items. I always make it a point to go over the checklist item by item, and at least half the time I find a few things missing. The charter companies are always embarrassed and usually make some excuse, but that wouldn't necessarily have been the case if you tried to tell them later than the missing items were never on board.

Contract

Review your contract for the following items:

Basic Terms: dates of charter, fees, amount of deposit, schedule of payments, pick-up and return locations.

Delivery: should guarantee boat is fully equipped and ready at agreed place, date and time.

Running Expenses: fuel (both engine and stove), food, drink, ice, dockage are not included if not specified in the contract.

Re-delivery: should specify in "good condition" with normal wear and tear. Should detail any late penalties. Should draw distinction between lateness and lateness due to act of nature.

UNDERWAY

There are two important items that you don't want to overlook while you're on your cruise: the logbook and the damage report.

The logbook is important to the charter company, because it provides them with necessary information about engine use, battery condition and other operational details. Each log will vary, but generally you only have to fill it out at the end of each day with the information they request.

Since the logbook is usually combined with your operational checklist, it also provides you with reminders of your various mechanical duties, such as checking the engine oil and water. Even more important is the protection that a careful record of your trip can offer in case you have problems or damage the yacht later. A complete and accurate log is always a reflection of your good seamanship. Make your log entries regularly as part of the daily routine, so you won't have to play catch-up at the end of the trip.

Since you'll turn in the official logbook at check-in when you return the yacht, you might want to keep your own log as a record of your cruise. You don't need a fancy logbook and, in fact, some of the most interesting logs are simply bound blank notebooks left for the entire crew to use. These end up as memorable collections of thoughts, reactions and notations, often illustrated with sketches or Polaroid photos.

The damage report is just what it sounds like: a listing of the uh-ohs that took place on your cruise. Damage report sounds more ominous than it is intended to be, and you should really think of it as what pilots call a *squawk sheet.* Obviously, if you drop a winch handle overboard, you should list it. But the damage report should also include everything from lights that don't work to portholes that leak. This provides a starting point for the service crew so they can correct the problem for the next charter crew. Once again, be sure that you note any problems as they occur so you don't have to wrack your memory after a week of sun, wind, and piña coladas.

CHECK-IN

It's been wonderful and you don't want to think about the realities of jobs, school, and winter snow, but the time has come to return your charter boat. Before you departed, your briefing probably covered the details of how, where and when you were to return the yacht and, if they didn't, make sure you ask. You'll usually return to the pier of your departure but, at other bases, there is a separate maintenance dock.

Before you reach the dock, your crew should have all of their gear and clothing packed in duffel bags and ready for departure, since you are expected to leave the boat shortly after it arrives to allow the shore crew to inspect and inventory the boat. In most cases, this is a quick process and you'll soon be on your way to the airport.

Your contract should specify when the company will inspect the yacht for damage, and it should be while you are present to prevent any damage occurring after your charter from being charged to your account. A lawsuit in the Great Lakes underlined such a situation. The charterer left immediately to catch an airplane; sometime later, he was billed for damage caused by a line wrapped around the propeller, which included a bent prop shaft and bearing replacements. He knew that the boat was operating properly when he returned it and, in court, it turned out that the company hadn't inspected the boat for several days, during which time it was used by some of the staff to tow other boats.

A recent charter with The Moorings in the British Virgin Islands illustrates how the check-in procedure can run smoothly. Using our VHF radio, we called the base as we neared the harbor of Road Town where The Moorings' base is located. At this point, our crew was packing their personal gear and clothing into duffel bags, checking all the lockers for forgotten items, and happily polishing off any food left in the galley.

Within minutes of arriving at the dock, our crew was able to get off the boat. The rest of the crew settled into the shade ashore while I stayed aboard with a Moorings check-in person. Since there were just the two of us aboard and the boat was tidy and gear was stowed, it took only a few moments to check the inventory list and make note of a few minor glitches. By the time our van was ready to leave for the airport, the check-in was complete and our deposit, on a credit card slip, had been returned and torn up. It was a painless ending to a delightful week.

9

What to Take

Overpacking is usually the curse of most charterers, even after dozens of trips, simply because you never know what you'll need. Indecision also enters into the equation, as does fashion, since you want to look well-dressed. The result is that you carry more than you need.

There is an apocryphal and oft-told story of a man whose airline lost his duffel bag full of clothing on the way to his charter. He purchased a swimsuit, two shirts and two pairs of shorts as interim replacements but, at the end of his charter, he found that he hadn't needed anything else!

On the other hand, in many areas, you'll need to take swimsuits for sunny days as well as foul-weather jackets for rainy ones, comfy clothing for sailing and dressy attire for shore. Even in the casual Caribbean, there are many resorts that require jackets and ties for men, dresses for women.

CARRYING YOUR CLOTHES

Soft luggage is an essential, at least on board the boat, since it has to stow easily into oddly shaped nooks and crannies. While many sailors routinely ship their duffel bags on airlines, I prefer to either just stuff mine into a hard-sided suitcase or repack when I get to the charter base, moving the contents of the suitcase into a duffel bag that was also inside. The empty suitcase is then left with the charter company, which has provisions for such storage.

I travel a great deal, and I've seen the brutal treatment that is given to soft-sided luggage such as duffel bags. I prefer not to arrive for a charter to find that broken containers of shaving cream, shampoo and other fluids have created an aroma embedded in all my clothing. I also like the security from pilferage afforded by hard luggage, although you can lock a duffel by putting a padlock through the zippers. Hard luggage also serves as protection from rain or dampness if the bags are left outside during loading of the aircraft.

Duffel bags come in all sizes, shapes and materials. If possible, get one with padded handles for easier carrying, as well as a detachable shoulder strap to tote them through airports. I own half a dozen big duffels, but my favorite is made of Acrilan (which is used for boat covers) and is 30" long by 12" in diameter. Admittedly I don't travel light, but this seabag has plenty of room to spare. The only other noteworthy features are a pair of zippered pockets on the outside for gear I want to keep handy. I've had duffels with inner liners, dividers, and even side pouches for dirty laundry, but the simple cylindrical duffel seems to offer the most flexibility in packing.

Whether they are rectangular or cylindrical doesn't matter, but don't pick a seabag too small. To support the load, the handles should be part of straps that extend all the way around the duffel, and the zipper should be plastic or other non-rusting material. Be sure the zippered opening extends from one end to the other for maximum access. The duffels in my closet are made from canvas, Acrilan, Dacron and even Kevlar, but I haven't found that one is superior to the others. One source for good duffels and other soft luggage is Land's End.

PACKING AND UNPACKING

Some sailors like to live out of their sea bag, and pack them so they resemble tidy dresser drawers. Others immediately unload their duffels into the drawers and lockers in their cabin. Either way you store your clothing, make sure it's in a dry location. Check drawers for watermarks that indicate previous wettings and, as insurance, you may want to line the bottoms with plastic trash bags. With today's shallow hulled yachts, the bilges aren't always deep enough to contain the bilgewater, which can slop up into lockers.

If you're carrying dress shirts, pants, blazers or dresses for shoreside use, you may want to invest in a soft suit carrier that can be hand carried aboard an airplane and stored intact in a hanging locker aboard the yacht.

Everything else in your duffel bag should be tightly rolled. This not only takes up the least amount of space, but it keeps the wrinkles out of sweaters and pants.

CLOTHING

What you wear is obviously going to be a function of where you're going and in what season. Fall cruising in New England, or England for that matter, is going to be vastly different from French Polynesia.

Regardless of your chartering area, you can plan on getting wet from an occasional rain shower or simply from spray. Take a water-repellent lightweight jacket or windbreaker, or a light foul-weather jacket. If you expect the rain to be more than infrequent, consider taking foul-weather pants and seaboots. For an early summer charter on Loch Ness in Scotland, I wore full foul-weather gear daily and was thankful I had it!

Even if you're sailing in a warm climate, don't forget the wind-chill factor, which can make the most sweltering day turn nippy offshore. For each knot of wind, the temperature lowers by one degree. For example, the tradewinds in the South Pacific regularly blow at 20 knots so, with an air temperature of 85°, you'll be feeling just 65°. With the boat sailing into the wind, the apparent wind might drop that wind-chill temperature to 55°.

At the opposite end of the spectrum, you need to consider both heat and sun. Sunburn protection consists of long-sleeved shirts, long pants, and hats. Cotton fabrics breathe best in the tropics, and you can find loose-fitting shirts that will keep you cool as well as protected. Light colors are obviously the best for reflecting heat.

Carry a pair of socks and underwear for every day, plus spares depending upon how likely it is you may get wet. I also carry spare athletic socks to prevent blisters from poorly fitting swimfins.

Layering is the modern approach to staying warm and dry, and modern fabrics now wick dampness away from the skin. Under a lightweight outer shell of windproof water-resistant fabric, you will find piles or buntings that are soft and comfortable in all conditions. By adding a soft shirt or sweater underneath, you have layers that can be added or removed as your body is warmed or cooled.

Take two swimsuits, so one can be drying while the other is being worn, and don't forget loose T-shirts for sun protection while swimming. I also take a pair of worn out sneakers to wear as foot protection while wading or swimming around reefs.

Be aware of local customs as you pack, because many popular charter areas remain quite puritan in their beliefs. Women going ashore in bikinis are often frowned upon, and men without shirts are equally offensive.

WHAT TO TAKE

One of the appendices is a checklist of items you may wish to take on your charter for comfort, safety, or amusement, including the following gear.

While every charter company offers masks, snorkels and swim fins, either as part of the yacht gear or as options, serious snorkelers usually bring their own equipment to assure a comfortable fit. If you wear glasses, you may want to invest in a prescription mask.

A camera is essential to record your cruise for posterity, and be sure to bring plenty of film. By the time you add up the cost of airfares, charter and food, a few extra rolls of film is a pittance compared to the increased pleasure when you return home. The basic

This boardsailer is an option chosen by this charter crew in French Polynesia, providing fun and a challenge when anchored.

camera kit should be a 35mm camera fitted with interchangeable lenses. I prefer to use a couple of different zooms, such as a 28-85mm lens for on-deck candids, and an 85-210mm lens for capturing more distant scenes. Use a clear filter (such as a skylight or UV) to protect the lens from scratches and spray. You'll also want a polarizing filter which can eliminate reflection as well as add dramatic tones to the sea and sky. A flash is useful for shooting inside the boat or in the evening. With today's modern electronic cameras, it's wise to carry a spare battery which may be of a type that you can't find in your charter area.

A regular part of my charter kit is a pair of polarized sunglasses with leather patches on the sides to protect my eyes from stray light. The polarized glasses can be vital for piloting in shallow water, since they allow you to see the various colors of the water (and hence the depth) more clearly.

A canvas tote bag is easy to pack, and you can use it for a multitude of tasks. I've used mine to carry blocks of ice back to the boat, to carry jackets and a camera ashore, and to bring back the booty purchased in local shops. Even on uninhabited islands, you can use the tote to bring back the inevitable shells, rocks, or other items that don't fit into your pockets.

Every charter boat is equipped with flashlights, but they're often bulky and heavy. For that reason, I always carry a small pocket flashlight, which I slip into a jacket pocket for everything from guidance while walking on dark piers to reading menus in candlelit restaurants. It's small enough that I can hold it in my teeth, leaving both hands free to struggle with a shackle or an outboard motor. But remember the joke that a flashlight is just a tube used for storing dead batteries. Always add new batteries before your trip.

FUN AND GAMES

This is a vacation, so don't be shy about taking a selection of toys for your own amusement. I always carry a stack of mysteries or spy novels, picked up at a used bookstore so I don't fret about the cost of throwing them away. Besides, they're great for gifts or bartering with the locals.

It is surprising that while every charter yacht has a good stereo system (some even have cassette disc players), the selection of tapes is uniformly abysmal. If you enjoy Beethoven, you'll find only heavy metal and vice versa. Take your own tapes with you, and also keep an eye open for tapes of local music during your shopping sprees. Some are awful, but many are good and will be fun to hear again at home.

If you're like most charterers, you'll be curious about the world around you, so take a few compact guidebooks to add some background to your cruise. A guide to tropical shells, for example, can open up new vistas in your reef explorations, or a book on birds can solve the everpresent "what was that?" question.

By the same token, a foreign dictionary or phrase book can go a long way to cementing relationships with the locals, as well as help you find the nearest bakery, liquor store, or bathroom.

Two packs of playing cards are a starting point for those ferocious evening games of hearts or canasta in the cockpit, or you may want to bring some of the travel-sized boards to play Scrabble or even Monopoly.

Even though I've simplified my clothing, I carry one of those little plastic sewing kits found in hotel rooms that has thread, needles, and buttons. When you've lost a button or a seam is starting to let go (from all those breakfast croissants), this kit is invaluable.

You can never have too many plastic bags with Ziploc seals. Take several different sizes, and use them to carry shells, extra or exposed film, spices, band aids, dirty laundry, wet swimsuits, your papers and money when going ashore in the dinghy, and a thousand other things. I keep taking more plastic bags, and I still run out because I keep discovering more uses for them.

If you are a yacht club member, you may wish to include your club burgee to fly from your yacht. I've done this several times, and it's always surprising to have someone row across to say they know someone in my club, or even to have club members arrive unexpectedly in the same anchorage. A tradition for yacht clubs worldwide is to trade burgees, so I generally carry a couple of extra burgees, and I've returned with the flags of yacht clubs from Ireland to Monaco.

To make sailing easier, I always carry a pair of sailing gloves that have the finger tips cut off so I can still tighten shackles, and they have reinforced palms for protection against rope burns. I also carry (in the ubiquitous plastic bag) a pair of old garden or work gloves, too. These are perfect to keep the slime and tar off my hands when anchoring, as well as for protection against sharp barnacles or coral fragments. A rigging knife is equally important, since it not only has a sharp blade for cutting, but a marlinespike for loosening knots and a tool for opening shackles. Keep it in your pocket when you're sailing.

This isn't exactly chartering gear, but I always carry several disposable ear plugs, purchased in pilot shops near airports, to block out screaming children or jet whine on the flights to and from my charters. In addition, I carry a soft eye mask to block out the light and allow sleeping in daylight during long flights (as well as on the charter boat when I want to sleep late!).

Seasickness remedies, in prescription or over-the-counter pills or ear patches, are important even if you're sure you won't be ill. You might want to include Kaopectate or Lomotil prescription pills to combat the spicy foods or uncertain water found in some areas. Sting kits are available in most drug stores, and they can ease the pain and itching from mosquito bites, bee stings, and other encounters with local bugs. If you are taking prescription medication, you should probably carry an extra supply as insurance, and an extra pair of prescription glasses can replace the ones last seen descending into deep water after you leaned over the rail.

For cold weather chartering, add a watch cap to keep your head warm, and gloves to do the same for your fingers. I like wool turtle knit sweaters under my foul-weather jackets, both for the warmth and for the anti-chafe protection around my neck. You might also want to include a terrycloth towel to wrap around your throat and block any drips from penetrating inside your jacket.

In the personal effects area, some charterers carry their own toilet paper, as many parts of the world use something about the consistency of sandpaper. Just be sure it is fully bio-degradable and suitable for holding tanks. Along the same thinking, I always carry several small bars of neatly packaged hotel soaps, which can be used if the local soap is unacceptable for any reason.

As far as paper and plastic money, I always take my passport which, even if not needed for the charter, always simplifies identification in any situation. Travelers checks are the best and safest way to carry money, and are redeemable nearly everywhere. Credit cards are also widely accepted, although it's always startling to buy something at a beachfront shack on a nearly deserted island, only to have them whip out a credit card imprinter.

10

Tips on Saving Dollars

Here are a batch of handy tips on how to keep the costs down for the charter cruise of your dreams. In addition to saving on your charter, some of these suggestions can also improve its quality as well.

1. Fly cheap. Investigate the reduced costs of night flights that not only get you to your destination on the morning of your charter, but save you the cost of a hotel room the night before as well. Explore the deals that ticket consolidators offer when they buy blocks of tickets and resell them at reduced rates. Before you book your charter, check with the airlines to see which days are the least expensive to travel. Flying midweek is often considerably less, and you can arrange your charter to fit the inexpensive days. Keep an eye open for the many two-for-one or companion fare offers from the airlines. See how many frequent flyer miles you have accumulated that you can use to save the cost of a seat. If you qualify as a senior citizen, the airlines often allow you to take a younger companion at the same price. Student fares can be used to reduce the ticket costs for your youngsters as well. Last, don't forget to check the price of your seats on the day you depart: you may have a refund coming if the price has gone down, but few travellers know enough to ask for it.

2. Pick your destination carefully. Sure, Thailand and Turkey sound like great cruising spots but, for the price of the airfare alone, you can pay for an entire week of cruising in the Pacific Northwest, the Florida Keys, or the Apostle Islands. Domestic airfares are not only less expensive, but you'll find more fare wars between airlines serving the same destination.

3. Save on hotels. You'll probably be arriving the day before your charter, which means you need overnight accommodations. Rather than breaking the budget with a resort hotel, see if your charter company offers sleep-aboard rates that not only cut your costs, but allow you to unpack and become familiar with your boat before the actual check-out process.

4. Plan your cruise economically. In the Caribbean, many sailors start their charters in the U.S. Virgin Islands and then cross to the British Virgins, where they pay $160 for customs and immigration for four people. By starting your cruise in the British Virgins, you have an immediate savings.

5. Shop the seasons. By chartering outside the high season, you can expect savings as much as 50-60%. In the San Juan Islands, for example, we saved $310 (almost 13%) by chartering in June, which is just before the summer high season starts. We had great weather, empty harbors, and no hordes of school children to contend with. By chartering at the end of the season after September 28, we could have doubled that savings (25% or $620) and still had the same weather and uncrowded conditions.

6. Compare boats carefully. You'll find wide variations in boat costs for the same number of berths, so do some comparison shopping between different boats (and different charter companies).

7. Anchor out. Commercial moorings in the Virgin Islands run $20 a night and a slip at Virgin Gorda Yacht Harbor is 90¢ a foot (plus electricity). Hang on the hook and save big.

8. Be stingy on fuel. Don't run at full throttle, but find a more economical cruising speed. And ask your charter company if you can bring your boat back with the fuel tanks filled rather than paying them to refuel—the savings will be considerable by topping up at a nearby fuel dock.

9. Enjoy happy hour on your boat. A Painkiller at the Pusser's bars in the British Virgins costs $6—a vast markup over the price of the inexpensive local rum. Besides, you have a boat with a view that most tourists would kill for. Sightsee ashore, but drink in your own cockpit.

10. Compare costs. Before you sign up for any charter, have a clear understanding of all the add-on fees beforehand. Some charter companies include the cost of a dinghy, an outboard, and all your bed linens, while others do not. In some cases, the add-on costs can actually turn a less expensive charter into a more expensive package than one that includes all the extras.

11. Be stingy with payments. Pay with an airline credit card so you are accruing frequent flyer mileage that you can use for your future airline tickets. A credit card also gives you protection in case of cancellations or problems with your charter. In foreign countries, explore the benefits of paying in the local currency, which may give you a savings over the U.S. dollar even after the conversion costs.

12. Bring your own equipment, such as fins and snorkels. Fins alone rent for $15 a week in the British Virgins, which is more than you'd pay to purchase them at a discount sporting goods store.

13. Skip the staples package. Many charter companies charge upwards of $15 per person for paper goods alone, which is far more than you'd pay for a week's supply of paper plates, paper towels and toilet paper in a local store. Condiments such as seasonings and spices can be brought from home in small quantities (35mm film canisters make great waterproof carriers) so you aren't throwing away expensive packages that have more than you need for your charter.

14. Take your own food. Not only does this save you shopping time and money when you get to your charter, it also assures you both of high quality and exactly the foods you want. We regularly ship a large Igloo ice chest as baggage, which I've fitted with steel hinges and a hasp so it can be padlocked shut to prevent theft. We shop at our local discount stores to stock up on steaks, chicken, cheese and other foods, which we then freeze solid for several days before departure. Even without using ice in the ice chest, the items stay frozen for more than 24 hours, which allows for your travel time to the charter. We don't have to worry that markets near the charter base won't have the foods we want, and we don't pay inflated prices to have the charter company provision our boat. By the way, don't try to ship an ice chest using dry ice. The airlines prohibit the use of dry ice, which may kill off pets in a cargo hold.

Part II
The Skills

11

Seamanship

This chapter isn't intended to replace any of the standard books on seamanship and boat handling, but there are certain skills that you'll need to manage a bareboat charter, and I'll touch on those here.

First of all, be willing to accept advice. If the charter company warns you against a particular harbor, don't go there. If they tell you not to go out in 25-knot winds, don't do it. And don't, unless it's a dire emergency, ever sail at night.

Second, there must be one person in charge at any given time. Since you'll be sailing with other people, you may want to rotate those duties on a daily basis but, at any moment, only one person should be making the decisions and issuing the orders. If you aren't comfortable with sharing the ultimate responsibility for the yacht with someone, you should make that clear before the charter is booked. Otherwise, you may find yourself in a situation where a life depends upon the correct actions, and any shouting match can only prove dangerous.

The first rule of seamanship is preparation, so you should make sure the boat is ready for use. On a daily basis, you should check the engine for oil and coolant level as well as belt tension, and also check fuel level. After starting the engine, keep an eye on the gauges for oil pressure, water temperature and charging rate to see that they are normal. Poke your head over the stern and see if cooling water is coming out of the exhaust.

In addition, you should plan to check the bilges daily to see if there are any leaks. You'll probably find some water dripping from the prop shaft, so pump the bilge dry daily so you can see if there is any abnormal amount of water entering the hull. Since fresh water is so precious, check the tanks daily and compare the amount used to the number of days left. If there seems to be a shortage, make sure the crew is aware they need to conserve fresh water.

Some rules of seamanship are basic, but bear repeating. Because chartering is a vacation sport, be careful about alcoholic consumption. It doesn't take many piña coladas in the midday sun to cause a serious deterioration of your response time and reasoning ability. If necessary, select a DH (designated helmsman) to run the boat without imbibing. Better yet, wait until you are anchored for the night before you open the bar.

THE CHECK-OUT

Your first test of seamanship is going to be a tough one, since the charter company will want you to demonstrate your abilities with a spin around the harbor. With the experience of watching hundreds of different skippers, they can quickly assess your ability and your confidence in boat handling. In a way, this will be similar to approaching a pier in front of a crowd of spectators...just thinking about the possibilities of error can make you nervous.

On the other hand, the check-out skipper isn't looking for perfect boat handling, particularly on a boat that is unfamiliar to you at this point. What he wants to see is a level of common sense. This might include your decision, even while being watched, to make a second pass at a pier when you think the first try isn't going to work out. It might be your resistance to being rushed through a quick check-out or your insistence on asking questions about everything.

Every check-out skipper is different, but they've all read your sailing resume and know your background. They may ask you to back away from the dock, pick up and then drop a mooring in mid-harbor, and return to the dock. Or they may have you take them for a short sail under your command. As the editor of a national yachting magazine, I was on and off hundreds of boats every year in the course of my writing duties, but I didn't get special treatment at charter bases and neither will you. Sometimes they simply handed me the keys and helped with my docklines, but more often I was put through the full battery of tests.

Start by briefing your crew on what you expect them to do. By delegating responsibilities clearly, you enable everything to take place with a minimum of difficulty and confusion. One person can handle the dinghy to keep the towline clear of the propeller, another can be responsible for tending the fenders if you're moored alongside a pier, and others will handle the bow and stern lines.

You should also alert the crew to what you don't want done, too. For example, if you've planned your approach to a pier perfectly, one crewmember jumping prematurely from the bow with a dockline can push the boat away from the pier and ruin your approach. You'll need to let them know which lines, bow or stern, should be cleated first, where to put the fenders, and what to do with the dinghy.

Be wary of pier side spectators, too, since they may know nothing about boats. More than a few yachts have crunched into piers when a line was tossed to someone on shore, who then helpfully pulled hard on it, which threw off the entire approach.

On your check-out as well as during the cruise, take everything slowly and don't try to show off.

PRIVATE TESTING

I have a first-day practice of going through a series of sea trials to *learn* the boat. Once clear of the dock, I stop the boat and back it down at various speeds to see how well it responds to the rudder and power settings. Because of the propeller rotation, most sailboats tend to pull to port when backing up, so you need to take this into account when planning your approaches and departures. If you need to back a sizable distance, one solution is to use power to get the boat moving steadily, and then put the engine in neutral. In this way, you can steer the boat easily in either direction, since the prop is no longer exerting any pull.

I also check the turning radius by spinning the boat hard-over in each direction. You'll find that, for the same reasons of propeller thrust, you'll turn tighter in one direction than the other, which may be of use to you in an awkward situation.

To judge the inertial speed of the boat, I find a buoy or similar marker in calm water. From a slow speed, see how much reverse power is needed to stop the boat right next to the buoy. This will give you an idea of how much power is needed when docking or anchoring.

By spending a little time to learn the traits of your charter yacht, you'll find that you're much more comfortable during the cruise as you face anchoring, docking or other maneuvering situations.

LEAVING THE DOCK

Until a boat is moving, there is no steering control, which makes leaving a dock more difficult than coming into one. If at all possible, try to power away from a dock going forward, since sailboats are not at their best in reverse, and you need as much control as possible.

It may seem foolish, but before you start any maneuver, you should count the docklines. A great many skippers, including famous racing sailors, have found themselves embarrassed to find that someone forgot to release the last dockline and no amount of engine power was going to move the boat.

When leaving, you can simplify your crew's work by *doubling* the mooring lines. In other words, run the line from the boat around the cleat or piling and back to the boat, so it can be released from on board. This eliminates the last minute clambering back aboard that can be awkward.

Decide on your course of action before releasing the docklines. To get the bow of the boat away from the dock, one of your crew can either push it out or, alternatively, pull in the stern to lever the bow away from the pier. The latter is probably the best course, since it keeps anyone from falling into the water. Be sure to use fenders to protect the hull from scraping the pier.

Spring lines can help get you away from a pier, especially if you're boxed in by neighboring boats. By reversing against a doubled aft spring line (with other docklines released), the bow will swing out into open water and you can then release the spring and go your merry way. Use a doubled forward spring line and power forward to swing the stern away from the pier. Either way, have someone stand by with a fender for hull protection.

DOCKING

Rule one for docking a charter yacht is to use the engine and have the sails down and furled. Rule two is to approach as slowly as possible, but with steerageway to control the boat. Brief the crew on where you expect to stop the boat and which docklines should be secured first. You might want to outline the procedure if you miss on the first approach, so that you don't wind up with one crew on the dock securing a dockline while the boat is trying to circle around for a second try.

Approach at a shallow angle, turning the bow out to swing the stern in, and using reverse to stop the boat as the bow and stern lines are passed ashore, or crewmembers step ashore. Note that I said *step,* because the boat should be close enough to safely step onto the pier or float. Too far out and your crew may wind up in the water if they misjudge or slip while jumping.

MOORINGS

Moorings are easy to pick up and leave, particularly when compared to either docking or anchoring, which is why mooring buoys are popular in many chartering areas.

Leaving a mooring is as simple as releasing the mooring line from your bow cleat, dropping it overboard, and signaling the helmsman to back away.

Just as with anchoring, you should be under power to pick up the mooring. If you're not familiar with the mooring, you might want to circle it once to get a good look at it. In most cases, there will be a ring on the top of the buoy with a mooring line attached, which you'll want to pick up using your boathook. If there isn't a line, you'll need to use one of your own, doubling it to return to your boat for release.

Approach the mooring buoy upwind and moving slowly. Your foredeck crew should point at the buoy, since it will probably be out of sight from the cockpit as you get close and, when the buoy is within reach, the crew should signal to stop with a clenched fist. When the line is secure, you can turn off the engine and relax. In some parts of the world, mooring buoys also have stern anchors attached so, after securing the bow mooring line, you pull up a stern line that is then secured at your stern to hold the boat from swinging.

In most tropical charter areas, a squall is easily visible long before it arrives, allowing prudent crews time to reduce sail and prepare for wind and rain.

Only when the mooring lines are secure can you leave the helm and shut down the engine, and there have been some fire drills when the crew relaxed before the boat was moored.

HEAVY WEATHER

It may seem obvious, but the simplest way to prevent problems from heavy weather is simply not to go out in it. Charterers, however, who have limited time and a pre-planned itinerary, often set sail in conditions that would make them think twice in their harbors at home. If the wind is blowing steadily over 25 knots, you're in for a wild ride and perhaps injury or damage unless you are competent and well-prepared. By the same token, it's not surprising that the competent and well-prepared crews are usually the ones who decide to spend another day at anchor rather than venturing out into rough seas and marginal conditions.

If you're already at sea, you should be prepared to shorten sail early. Waiting until your boat is overpowered just makes the job of reefing the mainsail and furling the jib even more difficult. Any time your boat is heeling more than 25 degrees, you're probably overpowered and sailing inefficiently, not to mention that the crew is uncomfortable.

In the tropics, you can see the squalls approaching from a great distance, with the tall pillar of black rain slanting upwards to the clouds. Before the rain is even close, the wind can quickly build from 15 knots to well over 30 knots, so it's the wise skipper who reefs the mainsail long before the squall arrives.

In preparation for heavy weather, be sure that all hatches and ports are closed and gear belowdecks is stored safely away so it won't fall. Wearing life jackets is a wise precaution, especially if you expect to be on deck for reefing or other work. A second towline on the dinghy is a good idea and you should probably remove any oars or other gear that might be lost.

Depending upon the severity (and expected duration) of the squall, you may choose to depower the sails before resorting to a reef. The mainsail should be flattened with the mainsheet to remove draft, and you can ease the traveller down to leeward to put a big bubble in the luff of the sail. The jib can also be depowered either by easing the sheet and allowing a similar bubble to form in the luff, or by rolling it up and reducing the sail area.

If you expect the weather to be unpredictable, by all means practice putting in reefs in light airs. You may discover a missing line and, at worst, you'll know exactly how to reef when you need it.

Most charter yachts have a *jiffy* or *slab* reefing system with a line through an eye on the leech and another line (or a hook) for the luff, and it's a good idea to keep both lines in place even in good weather.

Your first step is to tighten the topping lift to hold the boom up, and then ease the mainsheet to luff the mainsail. Lower the halyard enough so that the reefing line on the leech can be tightened to pull the sail snugly to the boom. At the same time, pull down the reef line on the luff (or put the grommet over the hook) and then rehoist and tighten the sail with the halyard. Ease the topping lift, trim the mainsheet back in, and you'll find the boat a much changed (and much more comfortable) yacht.

KNOTS

Everyone aboard should understand how to tie five basic knots: the square knot, the clove hitch, the double half-hitch, the bowline and the figure-eight.

A square knot, which is just two overhand knots together, is used to tie two lines of the same diameter together. The most common use aboard charter yachts is a version of the square knot called the reef knot, where you leave a bow sticking out so it can be untied by simply pulling the bow out.

A clove hitch, two loops atop one another, is used to attach dock lines to pilings or to tie fenders to lifelines.

A double half-hitch is an adjustable knot that slides, and is also used on pilings as a dockline.

The bowline is a reliable knot for making a non-slipping loop, and is used to attach jib sheets to the sails, as well as lines to other fittings. A bowline rarely jams, and is a good all-purpose knot.

The figure-eight is also called a stopper knot, since it is tied in the end of sheets to keep them from running out through the blocks. Tie it a few inches in from the end of the line so it has room for slippage, and use it in place of the overhand knot, which is hard to untie.

12

Anchoring

Without a doubt, anchoring is the number one problem for charter crews. Unfamiliar waters (and bottoms), unfamiliar boats and unfamiliar anchors all lead to dragging anchor and fouling other people's anchor rodes. Simply finding a suitable location with enough room in the usual harbor congestion can contribute to high blood pressure for the skipper and crew.

The key is planning ahead in every aspect of the anchoring procedure. Where do you want to lie? How much scope and swing do you need? Where are the anchors of the other boats?

As a charterer, you've probably anchored before and this isn't intended to be a comprehensive anchoring text but, rather, a look at anchoring for charter boats. Let's walk through some of the basics just so you don't miss anything.

One thing that you must make perfectly clear at the beginning of your charter is that one person, and only one person, is in charge. You may choose to change captains each day, but the captain at this moment is the only one to issue orders. Got that?

Unless engine problems prevent it, you should always anchor under power since you'll have more control and less other distractions around you. Some charter boats have two different types of anchors, a CQR and a Danforth, for example, and you should ask your charter company when and where to use each anchor for best holding.

Anchored off an island in French Polynesia, this charter crew can see the bottom easily, allowing them to check on their anchor regularly.

PREPARING TO ANCHOR

First of all, clear the decks for action. Stow the sunpads that clutter up the cockpit and foredeck, put away the soft drink cans and bags of potato chips, and coil down any halyards or lines that might get in the way.

One person on the foredeck should be responsible for handling the anchor and it's often beneficial to have the same crewmembers handle the anchoring every day. This doesn't mean sharing the responsibilities as well, but it does make for a more experienced team. At this point, the crew should unlash the anchor. If the anchor rode is a combination of chain and line, bring enough rode up on deck to be sure that it hasn't tangled from bouncing around during the day's sail. Chain is less likely to tangle, but you might want to bring a little up just as a precaution, since tangles are likely to occur on top rather than in the middle or bottom.

Speaking of tangled anchor lines, your crew should understand how to clear a snarl by opening the forepeak locker. As a safety precaution, the rest of the crew should do nothing to the anchor while this is going on.

As you enter the harbor, shorten up on the dinghy painter so that it won't wrap around the prop as you back down and, if you have enough crew, you should detail someone to keep the dinghy under control during the anchoring procedure.

For beginners and experts alike, picking up a mooring is the simplest and safest way to assure a good night's sleep.

The sails should also be furled securely, so they won't come loose at a critical point and block your vision or create steering problems. You should be prepared and have an emergency plan for all eventualities, including engine failure, snarled anchor rode, or crew overboard. If things are not going as planned, the best decision is to make a second pass after regrouping. Pressing on usually only makes a bad situation worse.

During one charter to Catalina Island aboard a Cal-46, I approached a mooring buoy and put the engine in reverse, but nothing happened. We had enough speed to get past the neighboring boats and, once into open water, I scrambled into the engine room to see what was wrong. The prop shaft was turning, the transmission was shifting properly; what could it be? Returning on deck, I overheard one of our crew comment on how clear the water was, and that you could see a shiny three-bladed propeller on the bottom! Sure enough...it was ours. The prop nut hadn't been properly secured and, when I shifted into reverse, the propeller spun itself right off the shaft. That's not a common occurrence, of course, but it underlines the need to be prepared for any contingency!

Since it's often difficult to hear commands over the wind and engine, work out a set of hand signals between the foredeck and helmsman. These should

Anchored for the day, this charter yacht has a sun awning rigged that also allows open hatches even during an evening shower.

be one-handed, since the foredeck crew may be holding the anchor rode with the other (or simply holding on!). In general, a closed fist means stop, a pointed finger means turn in that direction, a lowered palm or thumb means back up and a raised palm or thumb means go forward. There's nothing more amusing than watching a crew anchor in a flurry of shouted commands and frayed tempers, and a simple signaling procedure can make you look like a pro even on your first charter.

Power slowly around until you find a suitable spot that has sheltered water, good bottom for holding, enough depth even at low tide, and enough room to swing without interfering with other boats. Always approach the point where you drop the anchor from downwind (or down current if the current is stronger than the wind) at idle speed.

Stop the boat above where you want the anchor to rest and, when your forward motion is gone, signal the crew to lower the anchor enough to hit bottom. When it hits bottom, they can signal you to back down as they ease out the rode. When suitable scope is out, snub the anchor and check to see if it is holding.

Once you're settled in, it's not a bad idea to *swim the anchor.* As part of your afternoon swim, pull yourself down the anchor rode and see if the anchor is really set solidly. As a final precaution, take anchor bearings on shore objects

Once your yacht is safely anchored, the cockpit is likely to be the social center, but don't relax until you're sure the anchor is holding.

so you can quickly check to see if your position has changed. If possible, pick objects such as lighted signs that will be visible at night.

ANCHOR ETIQUETTE

Rule number one in anchoring is that the first boat in has priority. That means the first boat decides on the number of anchors to use and if everyone swings on a single anchor. The first boat also has first choice of any location.

As later skippers arrive after you, tell them where your anchor is located so they can stay clear, and insist politely that they anchor at a safe distance. You may encounter resistance and, if you're concerned, simply move to another location. You'll sleep better at night.

DRAGGING

If someone else drags anchor, wake up your crew and prepare to start the engine, but don't do it until absolutely necessary. Even then, use a flashlight to make sure that you won't tangle your propeller in someone else's anchor rode. If you can, simply fend off the other boat using fenders, but be very careful that you and your crew do not get your hands or feet between the boats. If there is a swell, watch out for rigging problems if the masts roll together.

Make note of the yacht name, type, and identification number as a precaution, even if you don't think any damage was done. You may find damage in daylight that you missed at night.

Last, be kind to the other skipper, because he's bound to be scared and upset. Everyone drags sooner or later, and someday it may be you in this situation.

If (woe betide!) it is your yacht that drags, get one or more competent crew up and start the engine immediately but leave it in neutral, since you may need power quickly.

Check the anchor rode to make sure that it hasn't broken or chafed through. If you aren't in immediate danger of hitting other boats or going aground, see if you can let out more scope to reset the anchor. Aside from feeling the anchor rode to check the tension, a boat with dragging anchor will pitch up and down, and the bow will hunt from side to side as the anchor skips along the bottom.

Evaluate the weather as you consider your options, since it may have been a wind shift that caused you to drag. If that occurred, is your anchorage still protected or should you find a safer harbor?

If you still can't get the anchor to stick, it's time to start over. Raise the anchor to water level and have your foredeck crew inspect it to see if it is fouled with muck or grass, or if it appears to be bent.

At night, be sure to switch on the depth sounder and look at the chart so you don't go aground while re-anchoring. Try to find another spot with a sandy or mud bottom that will provide good holding. Once re-anchored, take bearings on shore objects for position checks later. If the weather is turning unstable or you have concerns about the anchor holding, you may want to stay up for an hour or so as a precaution.

At dawn (which was 4 a.m.) during one Scottish charter, our placid mooring turned into a raging lee shore as a sudden storm approached, and we were literally pitched out of our berths and forced to head for open water rather than risk staying so close to danger. If you find yourself in the same situation, check the charts and simply find an area where you can sail around until dawn brings the opportunity to find a safer refuge. Don't try for another harbor or cove, unless you're absolutely certain of both your seamanship and your navigational skills.

RAISING ANCHOR

Once again, detail someone to tend to the dinghy and power slowly ahead, taking hand signals from the foredeck crew to keep the bow following the anchor rode as it is winched aboard. Don't use the anchor windlass to pull the boat forward, but simply to take in the slack; let the boat engine do the work.

If the anchor doesn't break free of the bottom, check to see if you're fouled on someone else's anchor. With clear water, you may be able to see that you're snagged on a coral head, and you can unwrap with directions from your crew. As a last alternative, use the stern anchor to temporarily re-anchor while you dive down to find a solution to the problem.

MED MOORING

Probably the biggest difference in European cruising (and some Pacific islands as well) is the so-called *Med Moor,* where the yacht is backed into the quay, secured by a bow anchor and stern lines ashore. An alternate method is to moor bow to the quay.

Because harbors are so small (and often overcrowded) this method allows all yachts to lie parallel to one another, separated by fenders, and taking up the minimum amount of precious quay space.

You might want to practice this before your charter (or during the check-out period with a charter company advisor aboard), but you'll get the hang of it quickly.

As with all anchoring procedures, the key is to brief the crew fully beforehand, proceed slowly, and not shout. In addition, Med mooring requires that you use lots of fenders, including at least one on the stern.

You'll need to have a good anchor and substantial chain, because European harbors are notorious for being deep but having poor holding.

As you enter the harbor, your first task is to choose your mooring spot. Use binoculars to select a space with convenient cleats, bitts or rings, and check to see if there are reasons the space is empty, such as a sunken boat (I've seen this!), a rock, or a protruding drain pipe from the shore.

The ideal location is lying parallel to the wind, so your boat isn't being pushed one way or another. Those spots fill up quickly (and early) in most harbors so, if you're arriving after midday, you can expect to find the premium moorings taken. Since many quays

Moored Med-style, these Swans are stern-to at the dock for easy boarding.

nearly encircle European harbors, you'll also need to decide between an upwind and a downwind mooring.

Everything else being equal (such as the distance to town or the proximity to a smelly fishing fleet), I prefer to moor with the wind pushing the boat off the quay. That puts less reliance on the holding of your anchor, and it provides a natural buffer that keeps your stern from tapping expensively into the quay.

If you're lucky enough to find a slot with the wind parallel to your mooring, simply round up and drop your anchor, then back into the available space. Most sailboats have rather poor directional control in reverse and often pull one way or the other (find this out during your check-out!). If your stern starts to sag off to one side, your anchor handler can add a little tension to the anchor rode to straighten the bow out.

If, however, the wind is off the beam, you'll need to drop your anchor at an angle to windward to hold your bow from being blown down on the leeward boats. Try not to anchor over the rodes of the other boats if at all possible, but know that it may be the only possible way. You can always straighten out things once you're secured and, in any case, you're likely to be the first to leave in the morning anyway.

With the wind abeam, your foredeck crew can maintain a light strain on the anchor rode to help hold the boat in position, although you may have to go forward and back in a crabbing motion to fit into your slot.

As you near the quay, snub the anchor and back down hard. With any luck, the anchor will dig in and you will stop short of the quay, but be prepared that the anchor may not bite, in which case you'll need to power forward and start over with more scope. Once dug in, you can release some rode to get the stern close enough to put a crewmember ashore with the stern lines (or you may pass them to one of the numerous bystanders waiting for you to make a mistake). If you have crosswinds, be sure to pass the windward stern line first.

In most European ports, you'll be securing to a bollard or a ring and, in either case, you should dead-end the stern line at your cleat and pass it around (or through) the bollard/ring and then back on board. That will make it easier for you to adjust for tidal changes without going ashore, and your departure will be simplified if you can slip the stern line as you power away.

If the bollards or rings are wide spaced, they will keep the stern centered properly in your mooring slot. If not, you should cross your stern lines so they act as spring lines to keep you centered.

Mooring bow to the quay is growing increasingly popular, especially as more sailing yachts have long reversed transoms that quays love to bite. As a result, many charter yachts have walk-through pulpits that make going ashore easy. Mooring bow-in is easier, since you can maneuver the boat better in forward than reverse, although you'll have to drop the anchor off the stern as you approach your spot. You'll need to rig a bridle to center the anchor line astern if you don't have a cleat in mid-transom. Otherwise, your boat won't lie parallel with the other boats. Mooring bow-in also gives you better privacy from the evening strollers on the quay, who otherwise can look directly into your open cabin, although I enjoy sitting in the cockpit in the evening and watching the passing parade.

Mooring bow to is also easier if you're shorthanded, since the skipper can pay out the stern anchor rode with one hand while steering with the other. Once close to the quay, cleat off the stern anchor and leave the engine idling in forward while you walk forward to handle dock lines. If the wind is across the mooring, just leave the helm turned slightly to windward to hold the boat up while you go forward.

When going ashore, move the boat away from the quay for safety by taking up some rode and easing the stern lines. If you have a gangway, fold it up for safety in case there is surge. A word of warning: many European harbors have regular ferry service, and these powerful ships can generate a surge that will bounce you around like a toy in a bathtub. Be prepared to move away from the quay when they enter the harbor, and leave your boat far enough away for safety when you go ashore or tuck in for the night.

When departing, you may be lucky enough to slip your stern lines, power forward over the anchor, and raise it neatly. On the other hand, you may also bring up one or two other anchor lines that have crossed yours. Good seamanship and common courtesy suggest that you should alert the other yachts to reset their anchors and haul in the slack on their anchor rode.

A few last tips on Med mooring. Don't forget to hang a fender over the stern (or over the bow) as well as over each side when mooring to keep the quay at a distance. If you think the harbor bottom is cluttered with debris or mooring chains, attach a buoyed trip line to your anchor to help with your departure (as well as to mark it for late arriving boats). Don't be afraid to warp the boat in if there are strong crosswinds or current, using the dinghy to run the stern line ashore after you've set your anchor.

BAHAMAS MOORING

Another anchoring style that is unfamiliar to most North American sailors is the Bahamian Moor, which uses two anchors to allow a boat to swing in a small diameter. Popular in the Bahamas from which it gets its name, Bahamas mooring is also used in areas of strong and variable current such as tidal streams or estuaries worldwide.

In essence, you will set two anchors 180° apart and position the boat midway between the anchors. Since you are leading both rodes from the bow, your boat is free to swing with tide or wind, yet moves only in a radius around the bow.

Most Bahamas mooring takes place in fairly shallow waters, so you'll have enough rode on each anchor to either drop back or power forward to set the second anchor. This allows you the choice of first dropping the stern anchor as you enter the mooring area and then powering forward to set the bow hook, or setting the bow anchor first and then dropping back to set the stern. The choice is dependent upon your own preference and the abilities of your crew. If you don't have enough anchor rode to set both hooks, you can simply tie the two rodes together in the middle and then power back to the mid-point after each anchor is set.

If possible, try to set the *line* of your two anchors slightly at an angle from the current, so that your boat will stay on one side of the rodes to eliminate the corkscrew twist that is the hallmark of Bahamas mooring. To solve the twist problem, coil one rode on the foredeck so you can pass it around the other anchor line as you depart.

If you need more scope to handle a temporary increase in wind, you can just ease the scope on one anchor rode as though you were riding to a single anchor. When the weather stabilizes, reposition yourself at the mid-point to keep your swinging circle at a minimum.

13

Navigation

For the most part, navigation in the chartering areas is easier than finding your way around a large city. If you have any qualms about your navigational abilities, courses from the U.S. Power Squadrons or U.S. Coast Guard Auxiliary can sharpen up rusty skills or add new ones.

Most of the popular charter areas are suitable for sailors with rudimentary navigational skills. The ability to plot a compass course, keep track of position, and read a chart are the most frequently required skills. In the Virgin Islands, for example, you are always within sight of land, although you may lose that contact occasionally during rain squalls. In Scandinavia, on the other hand, there are so many islands (and they are so similar) that you need to pay close attention to the chart to keep track of where you are in the maze.

Navigation in the Caribbean consists of watching for underwater hazards on the charts when cruising close to the islands, and plotting compass courses to make passages between the islands if the visibility is low.

For many sailors, part of the fun of chartering is the pre-planning that goes into deciding the itinerary, and this starts at home. You'll want a current guidebook for the area, and you can order these from one of the many nautical bookstores such as The Armchair Sailor. From reviewing this guidebook, you'll be able to decide on harbors or anchorages to visit during

your charter. Don't wait until you arrive at your charter yacht to start thinking about where you want to explore.

As you work out your plan of action, compile a list of questions to ask at the briefing. These might cover anything from the location of the best anchorages or snorkeling reefs to the procedures for entering a foreign port. You'll want to make full use of the local knowledge available during the briefing to check on sights, restaurants, hazards and weather conditions.

While doing your preliminary planning, you'll be selecting the places you want to visit and planning your route, but be sure to consider several factors:

1. The length of the charter
2. Crew ability
3. Prevailing winds
4. Tides and currents
5. The distance between harbors.

One mistake made by novice charterers is that they try to cover too much territory in too little time. A charter is intended to be relaxing, so rushing from one harbor to another can turn a vacation into a frenzy. Some experienced crews pre-budget one day as a spare, which they can spend at any time during the cruise when they find a place they want to linger or an unexpected area to explore. In many areas of the Caribbean, you may be sailing less than 20 miles a day, with time available for leisurely lunch stops or afternoon swims, before reaching your anchorage for the night. Trying to cover 100 miles a day is simply pushing too hard.

In some charter areas, such as Northern Europe and the U.S. Northeast, fog is an expected complication, so navigation skills are important.

The prevailing winds will shape your cruise, since you'll want to pick courses that are as easy to sail as possible. You'll probably find a few beats to windward in most areas, and scheduling those early in the cruise allows you to drift home in an easy manner.

The crew's ability should have been considered when choosing the area of your charter, and it should come into play again as you select courses. If the crew is new to chartering, don't set your sights on long beats to windward in the open sea, or you'll have a discouraged crew. Instead, try to break up any difficult sailing with stops along the way.

Seasickness is equally important to take into consideration. In the Abacos, for example, you can sail for miles inside the reefs and islands in perfectly flat water but if you venture outside, the seas can be steep and challenging.

Currents are a function of the tidal variation and, in the Caribbean and Mediterranean, the fluctuation is minimal so currents are generally weak. In the British Isles, Northern Europe and Scandinavia, planning your cruise around the tidal almanac can be crucial to reaching your destinations.

Distance between harbors is usually short in most cruising areas, but you'll want to keep safe refuges in mind just in case the weather changes suddenly on you. This isn't as critical in the Caribbean, where distances tend to be on the shorter side, but European cruising can expose you to longer spans between harbors.

Once your arrive at your charter base, you'll get the pre-charter briefing, when a company representative will walk you through your cruising area, using the charts found on your yacht. You should be prepared to take notes, because you'll literally be covering a lot of ground in this session.

COMMON SENSE

Since every charter company absolutely forbids any nighttime navigation, you'll only have to contend with daylight hours. Be realistic about daylight, too, because it can be very scary (and very dangerous) if you misjudge when the sun sets. In many charter areas, beacons and other aids to navigation are rather casual, so they may not be operational.

When the sun sets, it's often like turning out the light in many charter areas, so don't count on that lingering dusk that you get at home from the atmospheric pollution that glows for an hour or more after sunset. Darkness comes quickly in clean air.

If you aren't sure that you have enough time to reach another harbor, you don't. Stay where you are, and leave the next morning instead of putting your boat and crew into danger. Keep in mind also that if you have an accident while sailing at night, your insurance is invalid and you own the yacht.

EYEBALL NAVIGATION

In some areas, the water is so shallow that you have to consciously relax and not panic when the depth sounder reads just a few feet under your keel. In fact, I sailed for more than a week through the Bahamas with less than four feet on the sounder during most of the cruise.

Water color is the key to eyeball navigation. The paler the water, the shallower it is. Using your chart (which you should always keep handy in the cockpit), you'll get a feel for the patterns of shallows and reefs in the area you're transiting.

If you're concerned about a tricky passage, the best conditions for eyeball navigation are on a sunny day with the sun high and just behind you. Conversely, the worst time is in overcast weather, or with the sun ahead of you causing sparkle on the water. In fact, many experienced skippers simply won't attempt a difficult entrance in those conditions.

Polaroid sunglasses should be a part of your charter kit, since these lenses both intensify the color and eliminate surface glitter. With Polaroid lenses, you get an almost chart-like definition of the deeps and shallows around your boat.

Sand reflects white in shallow areas or a very pale blue in slightly deeper areas, while grass and rocks show up as dark blotches where you won't want to anchor. Coral heads are a yellowish color. As you tiptoe through shallow waters, you'll quickly acquire a knack for eyeball navigation, and it's nothing to be feared.

NAVIGATIONAL TOOLS

For the Caribbean, the depth sounder is an essential part of your navigational toolbox, and you should ask at the briefing where the transducer is located. If it is near the bottom of the keel, you will know that whatever reads on the sounder is your clearance from the bottom. If, as on most yachts, the transducer is located in the hull itself, you'll need to add in the depth of the keel to find out how much water you have beneath you.

Also for the Caribbean, a hand bearing compass can be useful for plotting position by using various points on the islands, a set of parallel rules will give you compass courses, and dividers will give you distances.

For European chartering, the above items are essential, along with either a radio direction finder or a Loran, which is usually called a Decca in Europe. With good radio beacons and Loran signals, you can use either to provide good position fixes when you're out of sight of land. Newer yachts may even have GPS units that lock onto satellites to give you a location accuracy of a few hundred feet.

Charts are essential to your cruise, and these should include overall views of the cruising area as well as detailed charts of the important harbors or anchorages. Most charter yachts will have at least one guidebook, and there may be a home-made guide from the charter company as well that duplicates your briefing.

Placemat navigation is a standing Caribbean joke, since many restaurants use plastic-coated charts as place settings, but more than a few sailors have navigated by using these miniature renditions of local harbors and anchorages. Don't put too much faith in them, however, because they're usually long out-of-date.

If you want to bring your own charts and guidebooks as I often do, contact the Armchair Sailor Bookstore (800-292-4278) for one of their 14 free lists of necessary charts and technical publications for various cruising areas worldwide. Just tell them where you're going, and they can provide the list as well as the items on it.

I generally take my own 7x50 binoculars which are comfortable for my vision, since I usually find that the binoculars provided aboard the yacht are corroded from long hours left in the cockpit.

AIDS TO NAVIGATION

Be sure that you are clear about which system of buoys is used to mark the waters in which you are sailing. There are two types of buoyage systems in use worldwide: lateral and cardinal. The lateral system marks the direction to a danger relative to the course that you should follow. For example, in the United States, we use the lateral system of *red-right-returning* to mark the safe channel when returning to port.

The cardinal system, however, indicates the direction of a danger relative to the buoy, and cardinal refers to the cardinal points of the compass.

In 1985, the International Association of Lighthouse Authorities (IALA) designated two systems of buoyage: System B (combined cardinal and lateral) which the United States uses and System A. IALA-B, with red buoys kept to the right when returning, is now in use in both North and South America, Japan, Korea and the Philippines. IALA-A, where red buoys mark the port side of the channel, are used in Europe, the British Isles, Scandinavia, Australia, New Zealand, Africa, and in some parts of the Caribbean and Asia.

COMMUNICATIONS

The VHF radio is your lifeline in most charter areas, and Channel 16 is used for distress and calling other yachts, but you should switch promptly to a non-priority channel for your conversations. In areas such as the Caribbean, most of the charter companies use a particular channel for their communications and, if you have problems or questions, they monitor that channel during the hours their base is open. Find out at the briefing about their channel and hours of use.

14

Dinghies

A good dinghy is as critical to a successful charter as food and water, but the dinghy can also be a recalcitrant child that you have to watch all the time.

Chartering around the world, you'll encounter a wide variety of dinghies and soon will become a connoisseur of the good and bad in small boats. In Europe, inflatable dinghies are popular because you are usually going to and from piers or quays, and their soft sides are easier on the hull of the charter boat. In the Caribbean and tropics, where you are often dragging the dinghy over coral reefs and onto beaches, rigid inflatables are the rule. In many areas, the older wood or fiberglass dinghies are being replaced by hard-bottomed inflatables, which combine the strengths of both types. This is a slow process, however, since hard-bottomed inflatables are expensive and charter companies are adding them only as others go out of service. Request a hard-bottomed inflatable if you can, however, since they are more stable, tow better, and are quieter when bumping against the hull at night.

DINGHY CHECK-OUT

Too many charter skippers concentrate on learning about their yacht and overlook the dinghy, only to find later that the oars don't fit or the outboard won't start.

During the check-out procedure, be sure that the oars fit into the oarlocks, and that they not only are the proper size for the dinghy, but also that both oars

Inflatable dinghies like this Avon are popular because they protect the hull of the charter yacht from scratches.

are the same length (don't laugh—it's happened!). One-piece oars are essential, because the two-piece style are flimsy and frustrating. With your check-out instructor present, start the outboard yourself to make sure that you understand any quirks it may have. Every dinghy should have a long painter for towing, a bailer, and a light anchor with enough rode to use on a reef.

The outboard should have a spare shear pin if it uses them, since you may bump the propeller on a coral head, and the outboard should be secured to the transom with a safety line in addition to the usual screw clamps.

If you have an inflatable, be sure you understand how to add air to keep it firm, and see that the charter company has left an air pump for that purpose.

DINGHY SEAMANSHIP

When boarding a dinghy, always step into the middle and sit down as quickly as you can to prevent a capsize. Never—ever—step on the gunwale unless you're

Watertoys such as this boardsailer are options offered by charter companies. In the background, a dinghy is ferrying a crew ashore.

planning to go swimming. Don't stand up in a dinghy either, even if you heard that George Washington did it on the Potomac.

You'll quickly learn the comfortable capacity of your dinghy, and you should be careful not to overload it, especially if the sea is choppy. You should also carry enough life vests for everyone in the dinghy.

Before casting off from shore or your boat, make sure the engine starts and is running smoothly, or you may find yourself rowing back against wind and current. Always carry the oars with you in the dinghy, for just those reasons. If you plan to use the dinghy after dark, always carry a powerful flashlight, both for spotting obstructions and for signaling if you have a problem.

If the engine on your charter boat fails, you can use your dinghy for power. Tie the dinghy amidships with both bow and stern lines, and use fenders to protect the hull. With someone in the dinghy to control the outboard throttle, you will use the rudder of the charter boat to steer. You can counteract some

With a squall fast approaching, it would be a good idea to add a second towline for security.

of the tendency to turn away from the dinghy side by aiming the outboard in the opposite direction.

Before you leave in the dinghy to explore, tell the crew where you're going and how long you'll be gone. This is not just common courtesy to keep them from being stranded on the boat, but a safety precaution in case you don't return on time.

BEACHING

Most good anchorages have calm water, so running the dinghy ashore is simple. Watch for rocks and coral heads as you approach shallow water. Aim for the spot you want with enough speed to shut the engine off when you get into shallow water, and coast ashore until the boat bumps the bottom. Step out and pull the dinghy up. If you can't coast far enough, use the oars to pole yourself to shore.

If there are breaking waves, however, beaching a dinghy can be a hair-raising experience. Every beach has areas where the waves are smaller than elsewhere so, as you approach, scan the beach for these spots.

In a perfect world, you would time the approaching swells and land between waves, quickly stepping out to drag or carry the dinghy ashore. I wish it always went that smoothly.

Since it doesn't, you should be prepared to get wet. Carry cameras or other valuables in plastic trash bags that are securely sealed. If you do capsize on a wave, keep an eye on the dinghy so it doesn't whack you a good one.

Once ashore, pull the dinghy above the high-water line, even if you only plan to stay for an hour. It's too easy to lose track of time and return to find the dinghy gone. If possible, tie the painter to a tree or rock, or use the anchor for added security.

Docks are simple compared to beaching, but be sure you leave enough length in the painter to handle the change in tide. Many charterers have returned from a day ashore to find their dinghy dangling from the pier by the painter in areas of higher tides. Secure the oars into the dinghy with rope, and don't leave any valuables behind.

It's an unfortunate part of life in the Caribbean that many areas have so-called boat boys, who are highly trained extortionists. When you go ashore, they offer to watch your dinghy for you, with the implied threat that it may be gone if you don't give them a few dollars. It's a good idea to accept this blackmail, if only for peace of mind.

TOWING THE DINGHY

You might be surprised (or perhaps not) to learn how many dinghies are lost while being towed. It's always back there bobbing along behind you until someone suddenly says, "Hey, where's the dinghy?" and it's gone. Part of the problem is that many charter companies use the yellow polypropylene braided line for the painter because it floats and is less likely to be wrapped around the propeller while maneuvering. But polypropylene line is both slippery and stiff, so it doesn't secure well to a cleat. I've watched as one of these painters slowly released itself, an inch at a time, from a cleat in spite of having two hitches on top!

There are several solutions: one is to knot the end of the polypropylene line so it can't slip past that point and another is to secure the cleated line by knotting it back onto itself. The third, and my favorite, is to use a spare dock line as a second tow line for security. That way you're protected if the primary lines slip or break, and you have an extra strong tow line in case the dinghy capsizes.

Before towing, remove any extra gear from the dinghy, including the outboard motor, which usually stores on a bracket on the stern pulpit. When removing the outboard, be sure you have a safety line secured to the big boat since this is a prime opportunity to drop it overboard.

If your dinghy swamps or capsizes while being towed, don't try to continue. A filled dinghy is a dead weight and can break the tow line or tear out the towing eye easily. If you can't bail out the dinghy, try pulling it up on deck using fenders to protect the hull, or rig the mainsheet on the boom as a hoist to get the water out of the dinghy before proceeding.

THE OUTBOARD

Outboards on charter yachts seem to come in two types: flawless and frustrating. Flawless outboards start with a single pull, run forever on a tank of fuel, and are light enough to lift easily to and from the dinghy. Frustrating outboards require a mystical chant to start on the twentieth pull, spew smoke and fumes, and weigh a ton.

Feeding the outboard properly is one way to keep it happy, and you should use the right fuel (usually 85 octane) and the correct fuel to oil mixture (usually 50-1). Check with the charter company for details, or ask them to supply an extra five-gallon can of outboard fuel with the boat.

If you dunk the outboard, either through capsizing or by dropping the engine, rinse it immediately with fresh water and then rinse it with gasoline several times. Try to start it promptly and, if it fires, run it until it is dry. Whatever you do, be sure you tell the charter company it was dunked, so they can take appropriate action and not pass it on to an unsuspecting charterer.

To prevent accidental dunkings, check the screw clamps on the outboard for tightness each time you use the dinghy, since they can vibrate loose.

STORING THE DINGHY

Where to put the dinghy at night can sometimes be a problem. With a little breeze, just tie it to the stern and it will float behind you all night. But if the wind dies, dinghies just love to come up to the charter yacht and tap gently on the hull next to your bunk until they get attention.

In calm conditions, you can tie the dinghy alongside with fenders but, if the wind or the sea comes up, it will thump enough to keep you awake. On larger boats (or with smaller dinghies), you can tie the dinghy to the anchor line, where it will swing around the anchor line without hitting the bow. Another alternative is to attach your spinnaker pole to a chainplate, aiming it outboard with the dinghy at the outer end, where it will circle harmlessly all night long. The drawback is that rigging up the spinnaker pole every night creates a tangle of lines, but you'll sleep soundly.

15

Safety and First Aid

SAFETY

Safety should be foremost in every skipper's mind, and a well-prepared crew always has a plan of action ready for every situation, whether it's a crewmember falling overboard, an engine failing during anchoring, or a flash fire in the galley. In general, emergencies occur with less frequency aboard charter boats than aboard the average private yacht, simply because charterers are more alert and haven't been lulled into complacency by familiar surroundings.

During the check-out, pay particular attention to the location of fire extinguishers (including Halon systems for the engine), life jackets, and shut-offs for stove and engine fuel. Your crew should also know how to use the VHF radio and what channels are monitored in your area, as well as the location of flares and other signaling devices.

Simple housekeeping can also prevent accidents, and you should coil all sheets and halyards neatly and promptly. It's easy to leave vacation gear such as jackets, swimfins and books, lying on deck, but they can also cause accidents, so tidy up regularly.

Crew Overboard

With most chartering in warm water, the dangers from hypothermia are minimized, but an exhausted swimmer can be in serious trouble, so immediate action is always required. In general, non swimmers should wear life jackets when outside the safety of the cockpit.

Particularly in the tropics, non swimmers might want to bring their own life vest. Called flotation aids, life vests can be found in styles that are comfortable to wear, not the bulky Mae West jackets that discourage use.

The five steps to a rescue effort are: first, stop the boat; second, get buoyancy to the victim; third, get the boat alongside safely; fourth, connect the victim to the boat; and fifth, get the victim aboard. Traditional methods of rescue have proven to take too long, and the current thinking is the so-called *quick-stop*.

As soon as someone falls overboard, the helmsman must detail someone to watch and point at the victim. Even in smooth seas, a head can be very difficult to spot.

The helmsman should then immediately tack the boat. It may seem dangerous to the sails or mast, but modern rigs are tremendously strong, and the first priority is to stay near the victim. If you are running wing-and-wing downwind, you need to let the jib sheet run free through the end of the pole and, if you are using a spinnaker, you simply head up while releasing the spinnaker halyard. The sail will come down fast into the water, where you can retrieve it wet but easily.

Once stopped, you need to provide buoyancy to support the victim. The fastest way is to throw a life cushion, and every charter boat should have one within easy reach of the helmsman, perhaps even in use as a backrest. Throw it slightly upwind of the swimmer so it will drift down toward the victim.

As you return, you need to plan to slow the boat alongside the victim so you can throw a line to the swimmer. During this process, shout encouragement, which can prevent the victim from panicking. Stopping the boat next to the swimmer can be tricky. You may want to head into the wind and stop next to the swimmer, or you can heave to by tacking without releasing the jib, which will allow the boat to move slowly at about one knot.

A line with a large loop can be thrown to both keep the swimmer from drifting away and to pull alongside the boat. Once the swimmer is alongside, the biggest difficulty will be getting him or her back aboard. Most charter yachts have swim platforms on the stern with ladders but, in any sea, these can be dangerous because of the up-and-down movement of the yacht. If a ladder can be rigged amidships, that would be best or, if you have enough crew, you can simply muscle the person back aboard.

If you have the opportunity, you might want to practice a man-overboard drill on your first afternoon sail using a life jacket or a cushion as a *victim*.

Keeping your crew aboard is just as important, and they should always wear non-slip sailing shoes when on deck, if only as protection against the many toe-stubbers found on sailboats. Remember the old adage "one hand for yourself and one for the boat" when working around the deck and, even if you're just lolling in the bow pulpit enjoying the spray, always hold on.

Fire

The galley is the most likely place to have a fire, either from grease or a flash-up from cooking. All of your crew should know where the fire extinguishers are located, as well as how to remove them from their brackets and trigger them.

Shout *fire* to alert the entire crew, and grab the nearest fire extinguisher. Spray it at the base of the flames, not the fire itself.

If the fire involves liquefied cooking gas such as propane, you should shut off the fuel supply immediately and let it burn itself out. You may want to keep nearby wood or fabric doused with water to prevent the fire from spreading.

Gasoline, grease or diesel fuel fires must be extinguished with Type B fire extinguishers. Don't ever use water, which will only spread the flames. Electrical fires should be fought with Type C extinguishers, although once the electricity is shut off, what usually remains is a simple wood or fabric fire.

Have a crewmember gather additional fire extinguishers from elsewhere on the boat and, if they aren't enough, send someone to borrow extinguishers from nearby boats.

If you are offshore and the fire isn't extinguished immediately, send a distress call giving your boat's description, location, and the nature of your emergency. If you are able to get the fire out, use the radio to cancel the distress call. If the fire gets out of control, you will have started a rescue effort.

Running Aground

As with all emergencies, don't panic. Running aground is something that all sailors do at one point or another, and usually more often than that! In the Bahamas, it's so common that it's called *bump-and-go.*

If you're under sail, you should promptly lower the mainsail and furl the jib to keep from going further aground. Don't worry about being tidy; just release the halyard and get the wind out of the sail. If you're under power, quickly put the engine in neutral and shut the engine off to keep from sucking debris and sand into the cooling system.

If the weather is reasonably calm and you've simply strayed a bit out of the channel, you have time to sort things out. If, on the other hand, the wind or seas are pushing you onto a reef or lee shore, there's no time to waste.

First, look for deep water, which will obviously be back along your path, but there also may be deep water nearby which is closer or easier to reach.

If there are no bottom debris in the water, start the engine and see if you can simply back the boat off the shoal. Heeling the boat by putting the entire crew on one side can help, and you can swing the boom out to leeward and let the crew sit on it to give leverage for heeling.

If heeling doesn't work, shut the engine down again to prevent overheating, and break out either the bow or stern anchor to kedge yourself off. You'll put the anchor in the dinghy and then row it out into an area of deep water. Carry just the anchor in the dinghy, and have someone pay out the remainder of the rode as you row away. Try to find a spot in line with either the bow or stern so that you'll have a straight pull, rather than trying to turn the boat as well as pull it free.

Once the anchor is set, use the anchor windlass to take up the slack and combine the pull with the engine to get free. If the anchor windlass is not up to the task (most aren't), use a jib sheet winch on the anchor rode and crank yourself off by hand. If you have an all chain rode, you'll need to fasten a sturdy dock line to the chain, and then lead the line to the winch.

If all else fails, set both anchors to hold the boat from drifting further into danger, and call the charter company for help. You may be approached in the meantime by other yachts or by locals offering to help, but be wary. Salvage laws are very complex, and you should agree on a price before any work is begun, or you may encounter legal problems later.

Flooding

If you discover that water is entering the boat, your first action should be to activate all the electric bilge pumps manually—don't rely on float switches which can jam open. Some of the crew can gather manual pumps or buckets, while the rest start a search for the location of the leak.

Unless you've run aground or had a collision, the most obvious places to look are the through-hull fittings for the head, sinks, or engine. Nine out of ten leaks are caused by a hose either breaking or pulling off the fitting, allowing seawater to gush in at a substantial rate. Close the seacock to stem the flow, and then re-attach the hose using double clamps.

If the seacocks and hoses are sound, you should check the stuffing box for the propeller shaft, the exhaust system for the engine, and any other openings in the hull such as a speedometer sensor.

One charter boat crew that suddenly found their floorboards underwater searched frantically for the source of the leak and it wasn't until a crewmember happened to taste the water that they discovered one of the freshwater tanks had sprung a leak, emptying itself into the bilge!

If you find that there is a hole causing the leak, heel the boat as far in the opposite direction as you can to keep the hole close to the surface, where the pressure of the water is less.

Use torn up curtains, sheets, pillows or anything you can find to stuff into the hole, holding it in place by wedging something against it (a floorboard? an oar?) from inside. This should stem the flow enough to allow the bilge pumps and your buckets to keep up, and you can make your way slowly to the nearest port for emergency repairs.

If you find yourself losing ground against the incoming water, and either can't find the leak or are unable to stop the flow, it's time to send out a distress call. As before, give description, location, and an estimate of how long you can stay afloat.

As a last-ditch effort, close the freshwater seacock for the diesel engine, and remove the intake hose from the seacock, putting it in the bilge. A diesel engine sucks an incredible amount of water through the cooling system and, as long as you can keep the intake clear of debris, it may allow you to stay ahead of the water.

Collision

The first rule when a collision is imminent is to make sure your crew doesn't attempt anything heroic. Keep your feet and your hands away from any point of contact, because the idea of simply pushing apart a pair of multi-ton yachts is absurd.

Your first task after impact is to check the safety of your crew and those of the other boat. A hard collision may have thrown people into the water, and they must be rescued before anything else is done.

Once assured that everyone is safe, assess the extent of damage. Has the hull been punctured? If so, is it above the waterline or below, where you may be taking water?

The collision may have broken your shrouds or damaged the chainplates that support the rigging. If so, rig halyards to help support the mast.

If possible, either hail or radio the other yacht to get the name of the owner and his address for insurance purposes. At worst, get the name, homeport and description of the yacht.

As soon as possible, radio the charter company and report the incident. They may want to send a boat to assist you, or they may attempt to track down the other party involved. Once you've squared everything away, you should write a detailed report for insurance purposes. Shock and time can serve to make your memory fuzzy, so get this done a soon as possible.

Wrapped Propeller

Everything is going perfectly and then, suddenly, the dinghy painter disappears under the stern at an amazing rate and the engine suddenly dies. The line is wrapped around the prop, a waterborne version of having your shoelaces tied together.

When you first realize that the propeller is eating rope, shift into neutral immediately. This will minimize the possibility of damage to the bearings or shaft.

It's sometimes possible to simply unwrap the prop by judicious use of tension on the line while the engine is shifted briefly into the opposite of the gear it was in when the line was wrapped.

If this doesn't work, it's time to get out the knife and go for a swim. Don't attempt to cut the propeller free until you're in smooth water, because the combination of a boat rolling and pitching in swells and a knife can be a dangerous combination. Once you've found calm water, a good swimmer should go overboard wearing a safety line tended by someone on deck. A serrated kitchen knife seems to work better than most rigging knives, but anything sharp (including a hack saw) will do the job. Simply carve away the line, being careful not to cut yourself in the process.

Once cleared, restart the engine and gently put it in gear. If you feel a rumbling or vibration, the prop shaft may be bent. Check the stuffing box to make sure that you aren't taking any water, and call the charter company for their recommendations. Even with a bent prop shaft, you'll probably be able to motor enough to anchor, although long distance powering is probably not a good idea.

Mechanical Failure

The two most common failures aboard a charter yacht are the refrigeration or the engine, and most can be traced to operator negligence.

If your refrigerator is suddenly not keeping things cold, perhaps you haven't run the engine enough to allow the compressor to work. If there is an on-off switch for the refrigeration, perhaps someone has accidentally turned it off. Aside from these simple remedies, your best solution is to call the charter company for advice.

Engine problems are more likely to be a result of operator error, and every charter company has endless stories about charterers who forgot to turn the ignition on at the electrical panel, or who left the master switch in the off position. Diesel engines are relatively bulletproof, so make sure that it isn't operator error before calling the charter company.

To keep from embarrassing yourself, check the simple things first, such as ignition switches, master battery switches, as well as making sure that the shift lever is in neutral, since most engines are prevented from starting in gear.

If the engine cranks over but doesn't catch, check the fuel flow. Is the fuel shut-off open and is there actually fuel in the tank itself? Bad fuel isn't an uncommon problem, so take a look at the fuel filter to see if it is clogged.

If the engine doesn't crank at all, are the batteries dead? Tapping the starter gently with a hammer may free it if it has gotten stuck.

If the engine was running and suddenly stopped, check the temperature gauge. If the engine is overheated, it may have a clogged water intake that caused the engine to expand and seize up. Clearing the water flow and allowing the engine to cool down may solve the problem, but be sure to alert the charter company so they can check for any long-term ill effects to the engine.

General Rules

Anyone left aboard while the rest of the crew goes ashore must have the engine keys and should know how to operate the boat. At worst, you should devise some sort of recall or alarm system to get the crew back from the beach if the anchor drags or something goes wrong. This can be as simple as raising the flag upside down, or as pre-planned as bringing a pair of handheld radios from home for just that use.

A basic rule on charter boats is that there is no swimming without someone else, preferably on deck. The buddy system is a proven method for staying out of trouble, and you should always snorkel in pairs and stay together, no matter how interesting the reef is over there.

If you're anchored in an area with current, it's a good idea to trail a line behind the boat with a lifering or floating cushion attached to it because swimming against current is a good way to exhaust yourself, especially in warm water. A line astern can be used to pull in someone who either falls overboard or doesn't realize how much effort is expended swimming in current. Warm water can be inviting, but don't stay in too long, especially if you aren't swimming regularly at home.

FIRST AID

With any luck, you won't even open the first-aid kit during your entire charter (except during the check-out, when you make sure it is fully stocked, of course).

Many regular charter sailors carry a Red Cross first-aid manual, or one of the many books aimed at nautical first aid, to augment whatever they may find aboard the yacht. Several such books are listed in the bibliography.

As a minimum precaution, several of your crew should have basic Red Cross courses, covering the Heimlich maneuver to clear an obstructed airway, external heart massage, and Cardio-Pulmonary Resuscitation (CPR). These courses usually include the basics of broken bones, bleeding, burns, and shock.

Preparing yourself mentally is just as important as having a complete inventory of medical supplies. Before leaving home for your charter, the entire crew should complete a medical survey that outlines any history of medical problems, with particular attention paid to chronic illnesses such as heart disease, asthma, diabetes, hypertension or epilepsy. List any regular prescription medications and, if a crewmember is on medication, he should consult his doctor regarding the impact of sudden withdrawal. If there are allergies to medicines, foods, chemicals or insect bites, these should also be included. In case of a medical emergency, such information can prove vital both for immediate diagnosis as well as treatment by a physician unfamiliar with the patient.

Sunburn

The biggest medical problem faced by most charter crews is usually sunburn, which can be avoided with some simple precautions. Charter areas are often warm and in the tropics, where the sun is directly overhead for much of the day. Bring an ample supply of skin protection, and make sure you wear it during the daylight hours, but particularly from 11a.m to 2p.m. when the sun is at its peak.

Modern skin protection comes in a variety of creams and liquids, but what you want to consider is the Sun Protection Factor (SPF) marked on the product. The higher the number, the longer it will protect you from burning. Sure, you want to go home with a tan to show off to your friends, but a sunburn can not only be painful, but medically dangerous.

One way to prepare yourself for chartering in the tropics is to go to a suntanning salon before you fly to your destination. A good base tan can go a long way toward protecting you during those early days of the charter.

Be particularly careful on overcast and hazy days, which can actually intensify the sun's rays. Don't count on the bimini top or awning for complete protection, either, because the sun reflects well off the water and can produce painful burns even in the shade.

Don't be fooled by cool breezes, which only mask the intensity of the sun in the tropics. Wearing a hat, with a safety line in case it blows off, and a loose shirt are your best protection.

Be careful while swimming and snorkeling, since water is no protection from the sun and an hour or two floating facedown over a reef can turn you as red as the proverbial lobster. Wear a T-shirt while snorkeling for protection.

Noses, lips and ears are particularly vulnerable to sunburn and, while there are numerous products specifically to protect these areas, the best remains white zinc oxide. Not only is it inexpensive and effective, but you can always tell when you need another layer.

Many suntan creams advertise that they are waterproof or stay on while swimming, but you would be well-advised to take those claims with caution. The exertion of swimming can cause your body to sweat even though you don't notice it, which helps to rinse away the protective layer. After swimming, add more sun protection.

Last, be careful about certain medications which can increase your reaction to sunlight. Ask your doctor if any of your prescription drugs create light sensitivity, and see if there is a substitute for the duration of the charter.

Seasickness

Unfortunately, another common malady is seasickness which is simply uncomfortable for most people, but can be incapacitating to others. In any case, it can ruin the day or even the trip.

Most people are aware that they may be prone to motion sickness, either through experiences in cars or airplanes, if not on boats. In this case, they should prepare themselves with medications.

In general, over-the-counter anti-seasickness pills have unpleasant side effects such as drowsiness and dry mouth. Prescription medications are more effective, and many sailors have switched to scopalomine, a drug which is released through the skin from a patch worn behind the ear. The drug also has the benefit that, unlike pills, it is not lost if the wearer does become sick. Another remedy gaining in popularity is a wrist band which places a small plastic dot on an acupuncture (the Nei-kuan) point to prevent motion sickness.

Any seasickness remedy needs to enter your system as early as possible, whether it is a pill or a patch, to give your body a chance to build up resistance before you test it offshore.

Even experienced offshore sailors get queasy, if not completely sick, so seasickness is nothing to hide. Be careful of your diet and stay away from greasy foods, questionable foreign foods, and too much alcohol (some vacation, right?).

If you do start to feel queasy, stay on deck and focus on the horizon to help stabilize your inner ear. A distraction, like helping to steer the boat, can also prove beneficial. If you are ill, use the leeward side of the boat (or a bucket) and be sure to hang on firmly. Nourish your body with fluids (no alcohol) and rest, and you'll soon be back on your feet.

Bites and Stings

Jellyfish, bees, and wasps are normally found in the typical chartering areas, so you should be prepared to deal with bites and stings. For jellyfish, Portuguese man-of-war or other stinging fish, do not use the commonly touted ammonia, alcohol, baking soda or meat tenderizer, all of which stimulate a discharge of the nematocyst, or stinging cell at the end of a tentacle. Instead, neutralize the toxins with vinegar or the commercial product Stingose. Antihistamines such as Benadryl and pain medication such as Tylenol or Demerol can reduce the pain and symptoms. Apply hot towels to the affected area.

Bee, wasp and hornet stings are marked by a small red area with swelling, itching and heat. If there is a stinger present, remove it gently and then apply ice to the area. Watch for a severe reaction, which is marked by breathing difficulty, nausea, weakness and difficulty in swallowing. If you have crew with a special sensitivity to insect bites, have them carry one of the sting kits available by prescription.

Medical Emergencies

The ABCD Rule is the basic formula for urgent medical crisis and, when injury occurs, you should survey the situation with these in mind.

A is for airway as well as control of the spine. Anytime there is a serious injury above the clavicle, you should assume there is a neck fracture. Clear the airway without tilting the victim's head.

B is for breathing. In addition to checking that the victim is breathing, be sure to observe the effectiveness of breathing, since chest injuries and rib fractures can impair the breathing process.

C is for circulation. Check the pulse immediately for frequency and strength. When you press on a fingernail, the color should return within three seconds if circulation is adequate. If there is external blood loss, control it with pressure.

D is for disability. Is the victim conscious and responsive? With head injuries, check the pupils to see if they react to light. Note whether they are small or large, and whether the eyes move in all directions. Last, examine the entire body for broken bones or other trauma that may have been overlooked previously.

16

Provisioning

You'll have a variety of options when it comes to provisioning your charter, ranging from a do-it-yourself effort at a local market near the charter base to a yacht completely provisioned from a list provided by the charter company. There are, of course, many variations in between, and most experienced charterers rely on such a combination.

After you've contracted for the charter, you'll receive an information package that will include a list of food and drink with prices. You'll also be provided a list of equipment found on the yacht, and you'll need to have both lists available as you plan your menus. You don't want to order the ingredients for a particular meal and find that you don't have the utensils to prepare that food.

Full provisioning is the least amount of effort as well as the highest cost. By checking off the desired items on the charter company food list, you eliminate any shopping when you get to the charter base, and the food is usually already waiting on board your boat in cardboard boxes for you to stow away. This is simple, but you're also paying premium prices for your ingredients.

Partial provisioning allows you to select certain items from the checklist, and then augment it either before you set sail or in various ports during your charter. In this way, you can have the charter company supply bulky or heavy items (such as cases of soft drinks or juices) so you don't have to tote them around an unfamiliar town while you

If you choose full provisions, your first task is to empty the cardboard boxes and store your food below.

shop. You can also select certain items where the charter company may have better connections. For good meats or vegetables, they are buying in large quantities, they use a supplier they know to be reliable, and they probably have the edge over your efforts at the local market. Partial provisioning also allows you to leave gaps in your meal planning for dining ashore or for discovering local foods to spice up your on-board menus.

Self-provisioning is the least expensive and the most effort. You buy only what you need and like, so there is little wasted food. On the other hand, your success at self-provisioning will depend on the availability of suitable markets close to the charter yacht, since you don't want to spend hours hunting for a meat market or bakery. In the Virgin Islands, for example, there are good supermarkets in St. Thomas and Tortola that have everything you need for provisioning close to the charter bases.

Provisioning your charter boat is a task that requires both concentration and imagination. You'll want to have a shopping list prepared before you arrive and one starting point for a self-provisioning list, of course, is the food list from the charter company itself. You'll need to remain flexible, however, in case a particular food isn't available and you have to make substitutions on the spot. If possible, key the foods on your shopping list so that you'll know not to buy certain items that were to be used in preparing a food that isn't available.

Once you've pencilled out a rough menu for the week, it's time to use your imagination. You don't want to be sitting peacefully at anchor, miles from civilization, and find that you forgot an important ingredient. Close your eyes, and mentally walk through every step of preparing each meal to make sure you have all the ingredients as well as the proper utensils. For example, "Breakfast is scrambled eggs, bacon, toast and jelly....oops, forgot to order jelly." Another scenario might be "Dinner is barbecued steak, salad, and baked potatoes. We'll need charcoal and starter for the steak, dressing and croutons for the salad, and toppings for the potatoes. Oops, we need to order aluminum foil to bake the potatoes. Do we have matches to light the barbecue?"

This galley surrounds the cook, with everything within reach.

When calculating the quantities you need, you should have a good idea of how your crew eats. For example, are they light or heavy coffee drinkers? This can make a major difference in the amount of coffee (plus cream and sugar) that you stock. Do they like one sandwich or two for lunch? Do they want mayonnaise on their sandwiches, or butter?

Keep in mind the second uses for many foods. Lettuce, for example, is usually included for salads, but don't forget that it adds a crispness to sandwiches on a warm day, and you'll need extra heads of lettuce for that use. Cheese is good for sandwiches, but be sure you have enough for snacks as well. Plan to make use of leftovers, too. Potatoes from last night's dinner can be turned into hash browns for breakfast, while chunks of meat can become tacos.

If you don't know an area, you should probably order a provisioning package to simplify your charter. After you've flown for hours and are faced with an unfamiliar town, perhaps another language, and a rapidly approaching departure, you may prefer to relax and simply put away the boxes on board. At The Moorings, 80% of their charterers order either full or partial provisioning.

As an example of provisioning packages, The Moorings offers several different options. The *Sail Away* is a

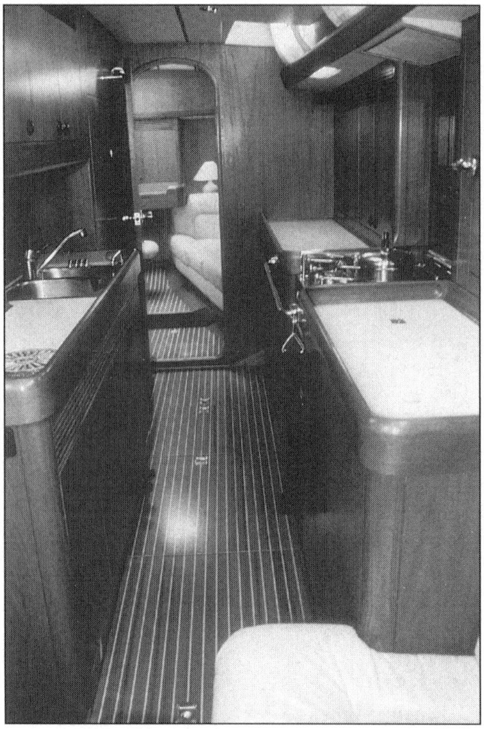

This galley is located in the passageway to the aft cabin which allows the cook to brace while sailing, but is dark and viewless.

complete pre-selected menu based on years of experience with what their clients like to eat (and are willing to prepare) during a charter. In this package, you get all breakfasts, all lunches, and an array of snacks and hors d'oeuvres for seven days. They also provide food for four dinners, assuming that you will eat ashore three times. This package includes everything necessary to prepare the meals, including charcoal for the barbecue and seasonings for the various entrees.

The *Dinner Ashore* package, which is only available in those areas where there are enough restaurants to make the program viable, consists of all breakfasts, lunches and snacks for seven days, plus one dinner.

The *Charter Starter* includes the basics needed for self-provisioning, such as spices, paper towels, soap, charcoal, etc. Custom provisioning, of course, is available from a multi-page list that can keep a gourmet cook busy for a week.

Regardless of the provisioning method, make sure that the entire crew is involved in making the choices of food. You should find out that one of your crew hates red meat long before the provisions are ordered or the meals planned.

One charterer, who regularly sails with different crews, sends out a preference sheet for foods before starting the meal planning. The list, in chart form, covers most of the meal possibilities for breakfast, lunch and dinner. The crewmembers then circle the items they like, and cross out the items they actively dislike. They can also number various sandwich fillings or dinner choices in order of preference.

In some locations, the charter company may stock their own provisions, in which case you can sometimes trade food from their packages. Before a charter in Baja California with The Moorings, for example, we swapped fish for chicken since our crew weren't seafood enthusiasts, and we also traded in several cans of pears for fresh pineapples that later turned up on spears in our evening mai-tais! Keep in mind that some provisioning packages are boring, leaning heavily toward steak and chicken every dinner.

One rule is to plan simple menus, because you don't want to spend all your time in the galley. Since you may be sailing at lunchtime, try to make the food one-handed so that the crew can eat it comfortably while steering or simply holding on. If you're undecided about lunch menus, remember the foods that you liked as a kid. I sailed with one crewmember whose idea of heaven was peanut butter and jelly sandwiches every day!

In addition, take your charter area into account as you plan the menus. In Europe, hearty breakfasts and late dinners are the rule. In the Caribbean or South Pacific, I prefer light breakfasts, a picnic lunch ashore on an islet, and an early dinner in the cockpit as the sun sets.

Take advantage of local foods, fruits and vegetables, too. Bakeries, whether in St. Martin, Scotland, or the Greek Islands, can provide wonderful staples as well as delightful dessert surprises. After exploring a small village in French Polynesia, it's nearly impossible to return to the yacht without a long baguette or two of freshly baked bread and perhaps an inexpensive jug of red wine. In the Bahamas, you'll have the opportunity to buy fresh conch and lobster inexpensively. In Greece, you'll have access to fresh vegetables, lamb and chicken.

The Caribbean in general is filled with lobster and fresh fish, but you can also sample breadfruit, mango, avocado, banana and key lime, to mention just a few of the local staples. Cristofene is a local squash that can be mashed like potatoes, batter fried like zucchini, or stuffed and baked like eggplant. Ackee grows on trees and has a custardy flesh that tastes like scrambled eggs, while Scotch Bonnet chili peppers hold the firepower of a dozen killer jalapeño peppers. Cassava is known to Americans as tapioca, and it can be boiled to a creamy pulp, fried into chips for spicy sauces or used in stews. If you want to try your hand at preparing some of the local foods, get a Caribbean cookbook.

The converse is also true: you can't find all foods in all countries. Although it surprises many people, you cannot find tortillas in Italy for your tacos, and you'll never see maple syrup in either Portugal or French Polynesia (where you should substitute coconut syrup, anyway!).

Every area has local breads, but most small bakeries don't use preservatives, so keep the bread wrapped and chilled until you need it. I've rowed a long way to bring back a sack of freshly baked warm croissants for breakfast, and you will too!

Sailing is hungry work, so you need to have enough snacks to keep the crew stocked with munchies between scheduled meals. Salty snacks are a good idea in the tropics, where it's important to balance your loss of salts, so make sure you have enough chips, peanuts, and dips. Peanut butter is a nutritious, high protein snack, and relatively easy to handle on crackers or celery, but it can be messy when it smears on cushions or cockpit sides. M&M's are better than chocolate bars, which can melt in your hand, not in your mouth. A mix of peanuts and M&M's makes for simple handfuls of snack, although you may find them in the corners of the cockpit if they dribble. You'll also want to have hors d'oeuvres for the cocktail hour as the dinner meal is being prepared.

Remember that chartering need not be the waterborne equivalent of a Boy Scout outing, at least when it comes to food.

I like chicken, since it is a meat acceptable to those who don't eat red meats and it can be cooked in a thousand ways. Chicken can be sauteed, baked, broiled, fried, made into kebabs, and barbecued. The leftovers from a chicken dinner can be saved for lunch sandwiches, used in a cool dinner salad, or made into bite-sized canapes for the dinner hour. We always orders boneless and skinless chicken because, after all, who wants to spend time in the galley boning a chicken?

The duffel bag of one sailing chef usually includes a selection of her own spices from garlic to meat sauces. She also brings powdered drink mixes to simplify the cocktail hour, as well as to add some surprises. Hiram Walker packaged mixers, for example, can greatly simplify anything from mai-tais to margaritas.

By the same token, she also takes packaged fajita and taco mixes for preparing sauces and meats. If you've ever tried to find such a sauce outside the United States, you'll know why it's wise to carry them with you. Besides, they pack flat and don't take up much room.

Just because you're chartering doesn't mean you can't have some decorative touch, so she always includes a bag of tiny umbrellas for drinks, long toothpicks with colorful tops for hors d'oeuvres, and colorful straws for sipping. Her duffel bag has also included party streamers and table decor, especially if a crewmember is celebrating a birthday or there is a holiday during the voyage, and she always brings a few linen napkins to mark important meals that deserve better than paper. She picks wildflowers from shore as table decorations, and always has a few candles in her duffel for a romantic evening meal. As a seagoing chef, that's hard to beat!

When it comes to beverages, you can't have enough. A tropical climate can literally dry you out, so be sure you have an ample supply of bottled water and fruit juices. Gallon jugs of water are the least expensive but hardest to pour while sailing, so order a couple of the handier quart bottles to refill and keep chilled. When figuring out the liquids for your crew, don't include soft drinks and beer because they won't contribute much to quenching thirst. Don't forget milk, available in jugs, cartons, or canned for long life, which can be added to foods as well as used for a nice cup of cocoa in the evenings.

On your provisioning list, you'll be offered every beverage from Dom Perignon to Coke, and you should be specific about what you are ordering and whether substitutions are acceptable to you. If you want Bloody Marys, make it clear to the charter company that they cannot substitute grape juice for tomato juice. We arrived at one charter to find that two cases of orange soda pop had been substituted for Coke, but luckily we were able to make a trade before we departed.

Alcoholic beverages are something that you can often find inexpensively during your voyage, depending once again upon the area. Local beers and wines may not be known internationally because they don't travel well, but you can find wonderful local wines in little European villages, and the Caribbean is notable for light and dark rums. Even in French Polynesia, where prices are sky-high for restaurant foods and grocery supplies, you can find an inexpensive plastic jug of red wine that is perfectly delightful.

In some cases, hard liquor may be overly expensive and you might want to compare prices with the duty-free shops on your flight to the charter base. In the Virgin Islands, there are often liquor price wars before Christmas, and you should always shop price if your first quote seems high.

GENERAL TIPS

After stowing your foods, put the cardboard grocery boxes ashore, since roaches like the glue found in the corrugations and get aboard that way.

Once you've opened a package or box of food, seal it closed inside a Ziplock bag to eliminate bugs, prevent any spillage, and keep moisture out.

Ice in most areas is a suitable substitute for gold, so carry plenty. I usually ask for a spare ice chest filled with bags of ice cubes, which can be stowed under the dining table or in the lazarette. Use the ice judiciously in drinks or to keep beer and soft drink cans cold.

If you expect the day's sail to be boisterous, you may not want to be down below in the galley while the boat is gyrating around you. Make up sandwiches in the morning, plastic wrap them for freshness, and store them in the refrigerator in a bag along with chips or nuts. When the crew gets hungry, you can send the one with the strongest stomach below to retrieve lunch.

Most charter yachts have areas set aside as *liquor lockers,* often with cut-outs for bottle storage, but you should be careful when stowing glass wine or liquor bottles. Make sure they don't clank into each other, and wine bottles should be stored upright to prevent leakage after opening. Some vintage wines suffer from disturbed sediment when taken sailing, so be selective in your choices. Champagne, incidentally, sails very well.

In general, try to keep all lunch foods (or foods to be eaten while underway) as simple as possible. A sailing meal shouldn't be easy to spill, leave the hands greasy, or take more than one hand to eat.

If possible, keep all the canned drinks in one side of the refrigerator, and the foods in another, since the crew will be in and out constantly. Try to put the drinks in a separate ice chest and restock it daily.

Wrap lettuce, celery and other vegetables tightly in plastic wrap to keep them from getting limp in the refrigerator.

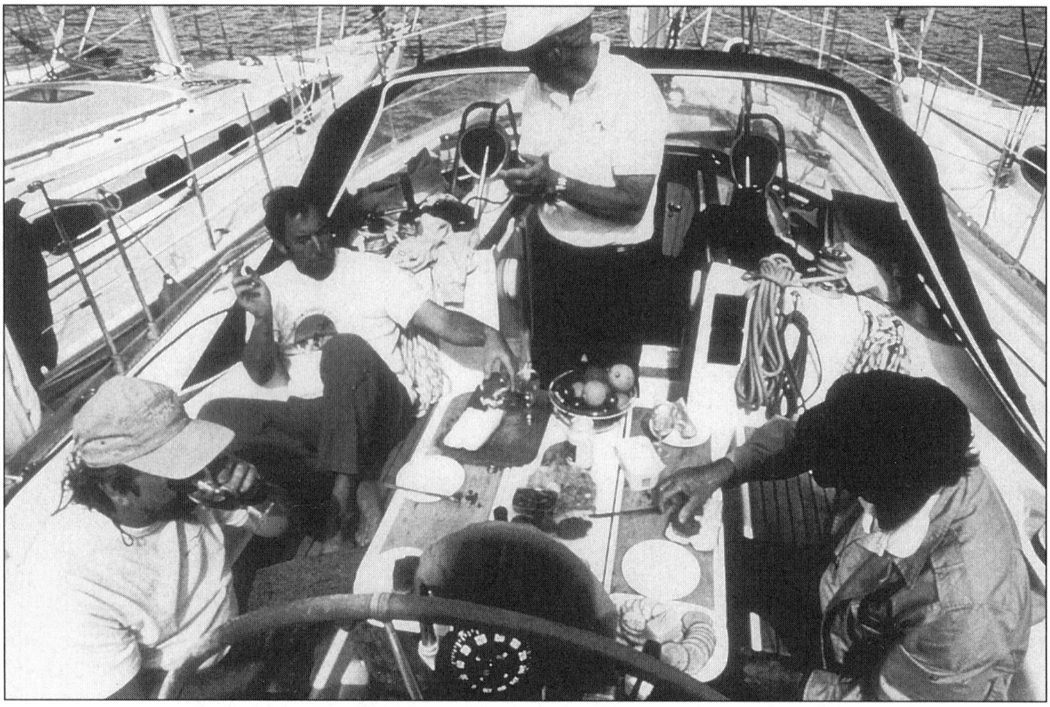

A permanently mounted cockpit table is a bonus because, in addition to providing alfresco dining, it simplifies snacks in the cockpit while sailing.

Paper plates simplify clean up immensely, but they're too flimsy for anything but sandwiches. Instead, you can use paper plates on top of your regular plates for strength and simplicity. An alternative is to bring a set of lightweight rattan paper plate liners from home, which are decorative as well as sturdy.

While using the stove, remember that even in a calm anchorage a passing boat can cause the boat to lurch, so you should be protected from splatters and spills. Use the fiddles (adjustable brackets) to keep pots from sliding on the stove. As one experienced sailor warns, "Don't fry bacon in your birthday suit," and that applies to skimpy bathing suits as well.

Carry plenty of plastic baggies in various sizes, not just for storing food but for saving leftovers and for freezing fresh-caught fish for later use. If you want special spices or condiments, put them in baggies and bring them from home, but be prepared to explain to immigration that the whitish substance is just garlic powder.

Trash bags serve not just to store and dump garbage, but they can keep your cameras and wallets dry when going ashore by dinghy. If you find the trash beginning to ripen, simply put the garbage bag in the dinghy to keep the yacht smelling fresh.

If you have favorite cooking knives, you might want to bring them from home, since you never know what you'll find aboard the boat. Some cooks simply bring a small sharpening stone, because they've found that charter yacht knives are uniformly dull from cutting lines away from propellers, cleaning fish, and other such treatment.

As a precaution, you might want to throw in a couple of rolls of mint-flavored antacid tablets, if only to combat those spicy meals ashore. Besides, you can always use them as dinner mints!

SAMPLE MENUS

Just because you're off cruising doesn't mean you have to suffer, and the following meals have proven over the years to be simple to prepare and a pleasure to eat.

Breakfasts

- Scrambled eggs, bacon, toast and fresh fruit
- French toast, fresh peaches with cream
- Cereal with sugar, milk, sliced bananas
- Potato pancakes with sour cream and salsa
- Omelet, croissants and fruit
- Fresh fruit, French bread and cheese
- Poached eggs, corned beef hash, muffins and fruit
- Pancakes with syrup, melon

Lunches

- Tuna salad, chips and salsa
- Beef tacos (leftovers) with cheese, sour cream, avocado and refried beans
- Chicken sandwiches (leftovers) with Swiss cheese and avocado
- Pasta salad
- Grilled cheese sandwiches

Dinners

- Steak barbecued outdoors, green salad, hot fudge sundae
- Roast beef, mashed potatoes, green beans almondine, apple pie
- Chicken breast sauteed in marsala, rice, green salad, chocolate cake
- Broiled lamb chops with red wine, potatoes, asparagus, ice cream
- Scallops, mushrooms, shallots sauteed in butter, squash, pudding
- Spaghetti with meat sauce, garlic bread, spinach salad, rum cake

17

Living Aboard

A charter yacht is not unlike a small mountain cabin or a beach cottage, and spending a week there in close proximity to other people requires some flexibility, humor, and resourcefulness. Privacy, silence, and water are often in short supply, so you should prize all three things highly. The remaining items in this chapter are also important for a pleasant cruise.

PRIVACY

One of the pleasures of a charter cruise is the ability to curl up in perfect surroundings and enjoy some peace.... from children, from work, and even from friends. Before you plop down and start talking to someone who is obviously engrossed in a book, you might want to simply remain quiet. By the same token, each stateroom is sacrosanct and, unless you've been invited to enter or asked to fetch something, stay out! Somehow, many of the common sensibilities found in homes are left behind on a charter, and you need to consciously respect the privacy of others. In a private home, you wouldn't walk unannounced into someone's bedroom, so don't do it on a boat.

Privacy also applies to other yachts and you must never, ever, board another yacht uninvited (except when rafted alongside). If you want to visit a neighboring boat, bring your dinghy alongside and shout *ahoy*, which gives the crew time to hide the dirty dishes before responding.

If you find yourself rafted up next to another boat and need to cross their deck to get ashore, always follow the same rules as you would at home. Use their foredeck (which is their front yard) rather than tramping through their cockpit (which is the living room).

Last, if you have rambunctious children aboard, plan to run the engine or generator often, or want to play your radio loudly, find an anchoring area away from your neighbors.

SHARING

Remember that a charter cruise is a group effort, so be sure to share in the duties and responsibilities whenever you can. If you aren't a good cook, you might volunteer for the galley clean-up duties, or you can make the lunch sandwiches. On a recent charter out of St. Martin, the mainsail was so hard to hoist that we ended up giving each male crew a *mainsail day*, when his task was to raise the main, but this also relieved him of having to help with the anchor (because he was too tired!).

CHILDREN

Bareboat chartering is a wonderful experience for children and it can be equally wonderful for the parents (and other crew) or it can be a frantic, noisy and harried existence with no escape.

Safety is probably the biggest concern of any parent, particularly on a sailboat with a variety of potentially dangerous equipment surrounded by deep water.

Your first step should be to make sure that your child is a good swimmer, which usually means Red Cross swimming courses at an early age. Young children should also wear life jackets on deck and in the cockpit, but they can be the comfortable vest styles that don't inhibit movement. Parents should also consider using a safety harness whenever the child is on deck while the boat is underway.

A basic rule is to always know where your children are on the boat. Under sail, bright-colored clothing is a good idea.

Show your child any potential hazards such as the anchor windlass, and warn them of the dangers in language that they can understand.

Because the parents may not be in command of the boat, be sure that children understand that the skipper's commands must be obeyed completely and immediately, just as though the orders were from the parents. As in any nautical situation, the captain's word is law.

If adults have trouble with sunburn, it should come as no surprise that children are even more susceptible. Long-sleeved shirts and lots of sun protection are necessary to avoid a painful burn.

Carry extra clothing, since kids are likely to get wet more often than adults, for whom that pleasure has faded with age. Spray from the bow is the seagoing equivalent of mud puddles, and you can count on children to frolic in it.

Children should also be given tasks during the charter, both to keep their interest and to involve them in the group activity. Trimming a jib sheet may be too much for their strength, but don't be afraid to let them try; it's part of the learning process. Besides, once they learn the loads that are involved, they'll be much more cautious in the future.

The one area that fascinates children is steering and, in most conditions, it's something they can do easily. They'll make mistakes, but your patience can lead to a fulfilling experience for them. Kids also like to study charts and delight in spotting buoys long before the rest of us with our vintage eyes. They can also help by watching the depth sounder in shallow waters, by coiling lines and halyards, and by tending the dinghy when everyone else is busy.

Kids will want to explore all parts of the boat, sit on the main boom, and swing on the rigging. Most of the time this is fine, but it may be too much during cocktail hour or early in the morning.

You should plan to bring a bag of distractions, such as a book of knots with some lengths of light line for practice, or they can play cards, checkers or with puzzles. A Walkman (with earphones, of course) and some story tapes suitable for the children can entertain them and provide quiet time for parents and crew alike.

HALYARDS

There are few sounds as irritating in an otherwise quiet anchorage as the bong-bong-bong of your neighbor's halyards slapping against a hollow aluminum mast.

Even if it doesn't bother you, your neighbors may not be pleased so be sure to tie your halyards away from the mast as part of the post-anchoring clean-up drill. In too many instances, a crew drops sail, lowers the anchor, and jumps in the dinghy to explore ashore without bothering even to casually tie off the halyards. These thoughtless types have returned to find all of the loose halyards pulled to the top of the mast where they were silent. The effort to retrieve those halyards usually serves to teach the lesson.

GENERATORS

Right up there in the same category as noisy halyards are noisy generators that run continuously. If you must use a generator, whether you are on a powerboat or a sailboat, use it sparingly. Cook your meal with the electric oven, chill the cabin down with the air conditioning, and then turn the generator off. If you must run the generator all night long, find another anchorage away from everyone else. There have been instances of charter crews going ashore and leaving the generator running endlessly into the evening, only to return to a yacht silenced by a potato shoved into the generator exhaust.

WATER

Water surrounds you, of course, but drinking water is a commodity that you must conserve carefully. Treat it like gold because, in many charter areas, it is priced similarly, if you can even get it!

Most charter yachts have shower heads that can be switched off once you have the temperature set. The procedure, sometimes called *Navy showers,* is to wet yourself down and then turn off the shower. Use your shampoo and soap to lather up completely, and then flick the shower button on for a quick rinse to remove the soap. When shaving, fill the sink with warm water rather than running the water over your razor.

In the galley, you're likely to have both a freshwater faucet and a saltwater pump that may be foot operated. Use saltwater for a preliminary cleaning of the dishes and utensils, and then rinse them in fresh water. You can also use saltwater if you need boiling water for thawing foods.

REFRIGERATORS

Because most charter cruising areas are located in warm weather climates, keeping food cold is a high priority, both from a health standpoint and from simply having enough cold drinks available. Many charter yachts will have a compressor-driven refrigeration system that operates when the engine is running, so be sure to ask during your check-out about the amount of engine time needed to keep the refrigerator cold.

Packing a refrigerator is a science and an art, but it's not difficult. The coldest area of the refrigerator is near the cold plates, so you should put frozen foods and supplies you don't need until the end of the cruise there. Be sure that frozen foods are wrapped carefully to avoid freezer burn, since some island groceries are rather casual about packaging. Re-wrap any meat packaged in plastic shrink-wrap, since it is too thin to provide adequate protection.

Open the refrigerator as infrequently as you can to preserve the cold. If you remove food that you plan to return to the refrigerator, do it as quickly as you can so it stays cold.

Many charter companies will provide an ice chest in addition to the refrigerator, and you can use this for soft drinks, beer, and juices that you'll want all day long.

STOWAGE

One simple rule covers every situation: put things away. This sounds like your mother nagging at you to pick up your room but, on an already confined charter boat, it only takes a few things to create a pigpen. Leaving towels, jackets, books or camera bags on the settees below or in the cockpit not only prevents other people from using those areas, but they can prove dangerous if someone trips or slips.

Before setting out for the day's voyage, secure everything down below, make sure that all the locker doors are closed and locked, and that there are no loose items that can fall when the boat heels to the first puff of wind. At the same time, close all the portholes until you're certain that there won't be any spray on deck. A wet bunk makes for a very unhappy shipmate.

As a matter of course, you'll be using the lifelines as a clothesline (did you remember to bring clothespins?) to dry towels and swimsuits, but these should all be put away before you depart, or you'll stand a chance of watching your dry clothes disappear overboard.

BARBECUES

Nearly every charter yacht has a barbecue mounted to the stern pulpit, since it's a perfect way to grill dinner while enjoying the sunset and cockpit conversation. But you need to take some simple precautions because, after all, this is an open fire.

First, make sure that there are no lines dangling nearby that can blow into the fire on an errant puff. Until you've seen a synthetic line catch fire like a firecracker fuse, you won't believe how flammable they are. The same applies to the bimini top and sail cover, which should be out of the way.

In a breeze, sparks can fly and, although your boat is usually safe since the stern is downwind at anchor, you may scatter sparks over yachts anchored astern of you, so keep an eye open for stray embers. Most charter companies insist that you use only charcoal and lighter fluid, but there's always someone who uses newspaper that floats off to leeward as a miniature firebomb.

If you can't seal off the top of the barbecue to starve the fire of oxygen after cooking is completed, then you should dump the barbecue into the water and make sure that all embers are out. An untended barbecue is an invitation to trouble.

BATTERIES

Most charter yachts have their electrical systems arranged so that there is one battery used solely for starting the engine, and one or more other batteries that supply the power for lights, refrigeration, water pressure pumps, and so forth. If you treat electricity as if it were fresh water and always turn everything off when not needed, you'll never have any electrical problems of your own causing.

During the check-out, make sure you understand the various positions of the master battery switch, since leaving it in the wrong position can leave you without enough battery power to crank the engine.

TOILETS

It is absolutely essential that everyone aboard understands how to operate a marine toilet, or head as it is called. During the check-out, you should have everyone practice flushing while there is someone present from the charter company. It is possible to exist on a charter boat without a functioning toilet, but it is not a pleasant experience.

Be sure that you have an ample supply of the proper toilet paper, since marine toilets are finicky that way. And don't put anything in the toilet that you haven't eaten first. It's that simple.

Every charter yacht will have a scrub brush and cleanser so you can keep the toilet clean, and this is everyone's responsibility.

To keep the head fresh, men should sit rather than stand when using the typically small marine toilets, especially when the weather is rough.

GARBAGE

You'll probably be told where to dump garbage during your pre-charter briefing and, if not, be sure to ask. Nearly every charter area has designated garbage collection sites, and it seems redundant in this ecologically conscious era to have to emphasize that no garbage should be dumped overboard. But both sailors and locals do it, and you can find trash nearly everywhere.

Carry a supply of large plastic trash bags with strong ties, and seal your garbage in these regularly to keep the cabin smelling fresh. There is often storage space in the lazarette or cockpit lockers to hide the filled trash bags until you can find a place to dump them.

Most towns that cater to charterers have dump bins near the docks for trash, but a few require you to pay a small fee to use them.

BUGS

You can expect to encounter various irritating critters of one kind or another during your cruise, so be prepared for them beforehand. Mosquitoes, gnats or the ubiquitous no-see-ums are particularly annoying at three in the morning when you hear that distinctive whining noise as they circle your face.

If you expect to encounter insects, bring a couple of cans of repellent spray from home that you have tested and found to be effective. If you don't expect to encounter insects, bring one can of repellent, because you never know when you'll need it. One popular cure for flying insects is to use Avon's *Skin So Soft* body lotion which, although it makes humans both soft and pleasant smelling, is apparently a bane to nearly every insect.

Roaches can also be found on charter yachts, although most companies have regularly scheduled fumigations to keep them to a minimum. Start with a dose of prevention, and don't bring any cardboard boxes on board, since roaches hide in the corrugations. Inspect boxes and can labels for roach eggs, which look like a dark blob of syrup about the size of a teardrop.

While there are a number of commercial roach sprays and poisons, the most effective aboard a boat seems to be a sprinkling of borax (such as found in Boraxo cleanser) in the bilge, locker bottoms, and in cabinets.

CLEARANCE

When entering a country, you need to clear through immigration as soon as possible. In many charter areas, this is a casual affair where you simply anchor off the nearest town and search out the local officials, whose offices are usually near the docks. Elsewhere, a more traditional method may be used. In some areas, you might need to call the customs or health officials on VHF radio and request that they come to your yacht, or you may indicate the same need by flying the yellow Q, or quarantine, flag from the starboard spreader after anchoring.

Requirements may differ, just as the formalities can be at opposite ends of the spectrum. Some countries require a typed list (in triplicate) of your crew, as well as a look at the ship's papers, all passports, and a copy of your clearance papers from the last port of call. Others may simply want to stamp your passports, and a few don't bother with any of this.

During your briefing, be sure to ask about the formalities for any foreign waters that you plan to cruise. If necessary, the charter company can provide you with the properly typed lists or forms required in each area.

FLAGS

It is common courtesy as well as a requirement in many areas that you not only fly the national ensign of the country in which your yacht is registered, but also to fly the courtesy flag of the country being visited. In some areas, officials (particularly in emerging nations) have become most inhospitable to yachts that do not observe this courtesy. On most charter yachts, you'll find an array of foreign flags in the navigation table, and hopefully they will be marked so you know which is which. The courtesy flag should be flown from the starboard spreader after you have cleared into the country and lowered the Q flag.

If you are a member of a yacht club, you can take your burgee with you and fly it from the starboard spreader if you are unable to attach it to the masthead in the traditional location.

MONEY

In most parts of the world, and particularly in the Caribbean, the American dollar is generally accepted, although you're likely to receive your change in the local currency, such as French francs or Dutch guilders.

Unless you're a long way out in the boondocks, traveler's checks are easily cashed, and I always carry two things: a wad of dollar bills, and some local currency that I converted at the airport or at a local bank. In that way, I'm covered for the miscellaneous costs and tips that come along.

When it comes to sharing the finances, you need to be clear with the others in the crew beforehand about how to deal with expenses. Certainly if you go ashore, you're on your own for food, drink and any other purchases. But what if you buy food for the boat?

I've found that a kitty in the form of a plastic baggie taped to the chart table can be the solution. Each crewmember puts in $50 or $100 at the start of the trip, and this kitty is used to pay for mooring charges, customs fees, for additional food, or even to tip the boat boys. When the baggie runs dry, everyone puts in another $50 to top it up. When the occasion seems appropriate, this kitty might also be used (by common consent) to treat everyone to ice cream cones or a round of drinks ashore.

DRUGS

Are you kidding? Don't even think about taking any recreational drugs on a charter boat. If you weren't thoroughly frightened by the movie *Midnight Express*, then you should remember that the only penalty for drugs in some cruising areas is execution. No appeals, no delays.

Part III

Charter Areas

18

The Caribbean

Without a doubt, the Caribbean is the most popular charter area in the world and, no surprise, every major charter company has at least one and often several bases scattered through this island chain. The Caribbean is a drawing card not just for Americans fleeing the winter slush, but for huge numbers of French, English, Italians and other Europeans who enjoy the international flavor of these multi-nation islands.

Your atlas will give you the details, but this cruising ground is essentially a long string of islands stretching through a crescent that curves east and south from Florida to the Venezuelan coast, forming a natural barrier between the Atlantic Ocean and the Caribbean Sea.

Because of the warm winds, protected waterways, and safe anchorages, this island necklace draws beginning and expert sailors alike. Chartering is a major tourist industry, attracting jet loads of sailors from around the world and, as a result, these are also the most congested charter grounds to be found. The only drawback to the Caribbean is that too many sailors know about it.

But don't let that dissuade you, or you'll miss an ocean full of treasures, ranging from tiny coral atolls to brooding foliage-covered volcanic islands laced with perfect beaches and harbors. In fact, a day's passage between many of these islands can bring a completely different culture: from British colonialism to Swedish architecture, from Dutch accents to American fast foods.

The Greater Antilles start just 90 miles off the Florida coast with Cuba,

Jamaica, Haiti, the Dominican Republic and Puerto Rico. East of Puerto Rico are the Virgin Islands, and then an open-water gap to Anguilla, which begins the Lesser Antilles. Stretching more than 400 miles to the South American coast, the Lesser Antilles were divided by the British into the Leeward and the Windward Islands, although more for governmental than geographic reasons.

The Leeward Islands range from St. Martin and Anguilla to Dominica, while the Windwards lie southward from Martinique to Grenada. In addition, charterers are beginning to explore the Dutch ABCs (Aruba, Curaçao and Bonaire) off the Venezuelan coast, as well as the reefs of Belize in British Honduras at the far western corner of the Caribbean.

Bear in mind the above names for the various areas, because you'll also hear a wide variety of other names that often seem confusing. The French Antilles are those islands clustered around Guadeloupe, while the Grenadines are the islands from St. Vincent to Grenada. OK so far?

Here's where it starts to get a little odd. The Dutch islands of Saba, St. Martin and Statia are sometimes called the Dutch Windwards, even though they are a part of the Leeward Islands. To compound things, St. Martin is often written as St. Maarten since it is half Dutch, and the islands of St. Barthelemy and St. Eustatius are usually shortened to St. Barts and Statia. You say tomato and I say tomahto. Don't worry about these idiosyncracies...just enjoy your cruising!

Weather: The prime charter season is the winter from mid-December through March, when most North Americans and Europeans are looking for escapes from winter snow and cold. The weather can be variable at that time, however, with rain squalls and stronger breezes.

For the Caribbean, northeasterly trades are the most common, ranging mostly from east to east-northeast. Windspeed in the 18-25 knot range are the norm for the winter months, while summer breezes drop to the low teens. The exceptions are the so-called *Christmas Winds* that often whistle up to 35+ knots on short notice. In general, you can expect the strongest breezes in the Windward Islands, and the easiest sailing in the Virgin Islands.

The best sailing season is from April through July, when the winds are lighter but steady from east to southeast, and the weather is more settled. Rain can be found year around, although steady rain is rare. Instead, you can watch the big cumulus build into towers and see the rain squalls slanting under each one, bring short bursts of heavy rain followed by rainbows and clear skies.

The hurricane season is theoretically from late July through early October although you can occasionally get off-season hurricanes. The hurricane season is usually the least expensive for chartering, with some companies offering two weeks for the price of one. Often the weather is flawless, but you run the risk not only of hurricanes but of fitful winds that can die completely, leaving you melting in high humidity.

The harbor at Charlotte Amalie in the U.S. Virgin Islands.
(Courtesy of the U.S. Virgin Islands Division of Tourism.)

Keep in mind that hurricanes are more likely to hit the East Coast of the U.S. than they are to rumble through the Caribbean.

While there are a number of reasonably protected areas (much of the Virgin Islands and the Tobago Cays), the other island areas are exposed to Atlantic swells that have been pushed all the way from Africa by the tradewinds, so the seas on many passages can be aggressive.

Books can (and have) been written about each of these island groups, so I'll skim over each of the major charter areas and suggest those sights that I've enjoyed.

THE VIRGIN ISLANDS

While the Caribbean is the most popular charter region in the world, the Virgin Islands are easily the most popular area within the Caribbean. Divided in half, with the U.S. Virgins to the west and the British Virgins to the east, this charter area is roughly 45 miles long by about 15 miles wide, so you can cover much of it in an afternoon sail.

The Virgins, both U.S. and British, are a first-timer's paradise, since the islands are close together which makes for smooth water sailing. The area is dotted with anchorages, many with mooring buoys, and the only drawback to the region is that it's too popular.

Spiced with tales of Henry Morgan, Bluebeard, corsairs and yellowed treasure maps, the majority of the sailing takes place in channels protected from the big Atlantic swells and navigation is entirely by eye, so the Virgins are an ideal spot to test your newly found chartering skills. In fact, you're never out of sight of land in the Virgins, and many of the anchorages are within a few miles of each other, leaving plenty of time to explore or sail before anchoring for the night. The water is clear to remarkable depths, and the weather is generally settled.

The British Virgins (usually called BVI) have more charter boats than the American islands, with several large companies based on Tortola, which is centrally located in the middle of the chain. In fact, The Moorings advertises that more than 16 anchorages are within a one hour's sail from their marina in Road Town, and an equal number are probably within reach of other charter company bases at Red Hook or East End.

On a typical itinerary from Tortola, many boats start their cruises by reaching south across Sir Francis Drake Channel to The Bight on Norman Island, a completely protected anchorage with a good breeze for air conditioning. As a result, The Bight is often congested but still worth a visit, since nearby caves are said to be those described in Robert Louis Stevenson's *Treasure Island* and, in fact, treasure has been found in the area.

Virgin Gorda is another popular sight on the charter trail, particularly The Baths at the southern tip, a giant's playground of huge boulders tumbled over each other at the water's edge. The result is a series of interconnected grottoes of cool, clear water, marked by intricate patterns of sunlight shining through gaps in the boulders and reflecting around the pools. Since The Baths can often be overrun by tourists and other charter yachts, you might prefer nearby Devil's Bay, which has similar boulders, a nicer beach, and no crowds.

At the opposite end of the island is Gorda Sound, another protected area with numerous anchorages as well as a collection of excellent restaurants for evening dining. Also located in Gorda Sound and accessible only by water is the Bitter End Yacht Club, a private resort that welcomes sailors.

On the Atlantic side of Tortola is Cane Garden Bay, said to be the prettiest cove in the world, which is an excellent anchorage except in northerly winds. Be sure to try Stanley Hodges' Welcome Bar and Restaurant for great lobster, music and rum drinks. Nearby is the Callwood distillery, where you can sample the island rum but, beware, it's strong stuff!

For divers or snorkelers, try Salt Island, where the Royal Mail Ship *Rhone* sank during a storm in 1876 and whose remains are now a condo for brightly colored fish.

Moorings have been set by a private firm both as a commercial operation and to help protect the coral reefs which have been damaged by inconsiderate anchoring. The moorings, which cost

$20 per night, are located at Cooper Island, Drake's Anchorage and Vixen Point in Virgin Gorda's North Sound, Cane Garden Bay, Soper's Hole, and in two areas of Little Harbor on Jost van Dyke.

The U.S. Virgin Islands were acquired from the Danes in 1917 and parts of it still retain a European flavor, including the startling habit of driving on the left. The capital, Charlotte Amalie, is packed to bursting with cruise ships and tourists, however, and crime is becoming enough of a problem that most charter boats not based in the harbor tend to skip this city. It is also a slice of Americana, including fast foods such as Kentucky Fried Chicken and shops filled with tourist junk, from which most charterers are trying to escape.

Red Hook Bay on the east side of St. Thomas is a major charter base and is a convenient starting point for exploring the British Virgins. Be sure to clear customs on the way out and back, or you'll pay a fine.

Nearby St. John is often overlooked by sailors in a hurry to reach the British Virgins, but it offers some delights of its own. Most of it is a National Park, so it remains untouched and original, and the rest of the island is equally distant from the twentieth century. Cruz Bay, where you'll clear customs, is often congested, but Pusser's Pub, which serves rum of the same name, is both nautical and scenic. Caneel Bay on the north side of the island is a posh Rockefeller resort that requires coats and ties, so many charterers skip that area, but you might try Honeymoon Beach just west of Caneel Bay, where tame manta rays are often found playing near the beach. Another prime snorkeling area is Haulover Bay at the eastern tip of St. John's, with giant pillars of elkhorn coral heads.

THE LEEWARD ISLANDS

Made up of the primary islands of St. Martin, Anguilla, St. Barts, St. Kitts, Guadeloupe and Dominica, plus a collection of smaller islets, this is a fascinating mix of British, Dutch, French and West Indian cultures. Because sailing the Leewards involves some open water passages that can be challenging, this area requires more experienced sailors than the Virgins. Because it involved an often nasty beat in sloppy head seas from the Virgin Islands, the northernmost of the Leewards were late bloomers in the charter business.

St. Martin/St. Maarten is a unique combination of Paris and Amsterdam spiced with West Indian rhythms. Discovered by Columbus, it was a battlefield until the seventeenth century when the two nations agreed to split the island in half. Several major charter operations are based here, and among the spectacular anchorages are Simpson Bay, Marcel Bay, Grand Case, Orient Bay and many others. Marigot, the French capital, has chic shops and waterfront cafes where you can munch on a croissant and stock up on red wines. The Dutch capital, Philipsburg, also has shopping, casinos and nightlife, but the anchorage is often too lumpy for comfortable overnighting. St. Martin has become one of the largest charter bases

Somewhere in this mound of conch shells, you'll find the perfect souvenir of Anguilla's conch lady.

in the Caribbean, in part because the French offered tremendous tax advantages to those who invest in charter boats.

Anguilla, just five miles away, remains British and this low coral island is largely undeveloped, so the white sand beaches and offshore reefs remain unspoiled. Road Bay is a pleasant anchorage, although you'll hear all the revelry at Johnny O's on the beach. Don't miss out on the conch lady at the end of the beach, who literally has a mountain of conch shells for sale at reasonable prices. At nearby Prickly Pear Cays, you'll find some of the best snorkeling in the Caribbean, with several sunken ships to spice up the view. Sandy Cay, just offshore from Road Bay, is everyone's idea of a tiny tropical island, and you can pick up a mooring outside the reef for a daytime stop, although it's usually too rolly for overnighting. There's a tiny snack bar ashore, and an inviting reef that surrounds the palm-fringed islet. Anguilla has instituted a rather hefty cruising fee on charter yachts that ranges up to $125, depending upon the size of the yacht. Check with your charter company to see if the fee has been paid by them or repealed.

St. Barts is French, and has become a jet set destination, which hasn't helped prices or service particularly. Named by Columbus for his brother, it has a couple of good anchorages. The port of

Gustavia on the west coast is protected and charming, but often packed to the gills with visiting yachts paying $14 to Med-moor to the quay. Because it is so sheltered, however, it can also be hot and humid. Food is a way of life to the French, so tiny St. Barts, with a population of just 3000, has more than 70 restaurants, and you can also find jazz and dancing until the wee hours. As a bonus, the French officials are happy and helpful.

Saba is about 25 miles southwest of St. Martin but rarely visited by charter yachts because it has no harbors and, to land, you must pick very calm weather to use the pier.

Statia is pretty, with clouds usually snagged on its peak, but has little to draw charterers since the anchorages are open and lumpy. St. Kitts and Nevis are pretty too, but also have uncomfortable anchorages.

Antigua was where chartering began in the Caribbean, with yachts based at English Harbour, so-named because Lord Nelson kept his British fleet here while colonizing North America. That British flavor remains, from the cannons on display to the seawall filled with yachts.

Each spring, Antigua hosts the Antigua Race Week, an event that draws sailors and camp-followers from around the world to a week of offshore sailing and on-shore high jinks. Unless you plan to sail or participate in the wet T-shirt contests, this is a good time to stay away from Antigua because of the crowds and high prices.

Try to arrive in English Harbour on a Sunday, because the entire island seems to cab or hike up to Shirley Heights for the sunset and view of other islands, and then to enjoy cocktails and a barbecue, followed by steel bands and reggae music.

There's more to Antigua than just English Harbour, however, and locals claim that the island has one beach for every day of the year. There are also a number of pleasant coves and anchorages, and some charterers never leave the island, contenting themselves to simply cruise from one anchorage to another. Good anchorages include Five Islands, Deep Bay, Mosquito Cove, and Dickenson Bay. Sailing along the leeward side is unforgettable, with good breezes, no swells, and crystal clear water that reveals the bottom 30 feet below.

Guadeloupe is actually two islands, Basse Terre and Grande Terre, that are connected by a drawbridge. Basse Terre has a lush 60,000-acre national park complete with a 300-foot waterfall as well as an underwater park (near Pigeon Island) named by Jacques Cousteau as one of the world's 10 best diving areas. Just south are Les Saintes (The Saints), a cluster of islands that have become a popular vacation spot for local residents, so the anchorages are sometimes crowded and rumpled by passing ferries.

A 4-5 hour sail from Guadeloupe, Dominica is one of the most exotic of the Caribbean islands, with a lush tropical rainforest, bamboo forests, and a mountain that towers more than a mile high. You can easily spend a day with a local guide exploring the interior of the island, since there are more than 350 rivers and spectacular scenery. It also has

fewer harbors than other islands, although the best is Prince Rupert Bay. A word of warning, however, the geography at the entrance to the harbor creates some ferocious wind gusts, although the seas remain smooth. You'll also find boats full of boys who insist on helping you. Once you've picked your boy (negotiate all fees beforehand!), he'll chase the others away, watch your boat for you, and deliver ice or fruit from shore. He may also offer to lead you up Indian River by dinghy, which is a fun trip into a lush jungle where you can swim in clear freshwater.

THE WINDWARD ISLANDS

Martinique is another base for charter operators, and this big French island is topped by Mont Pelée at the south end, a hulking volcano that wiped out a town of 40,000 (except one prisoner in the dungeon!) with an eruption in 1902. The largest city, Fort-de-France, is a favorite stop for cruise ships, so the bay can be lumpy and crowded. Sainte Anne is a pleasant little town with a good anchorage as well as shops and restaurants. Anse d'Arlet is a lovely anchorage in front of a French fishing village, and Anse Mitan has beach restaurants and a casino.

St. Lucia is also a charter base, and James Michener called Marigot Bay "the most beautiful bay in the Caribbean." Equally beautiful are The Pitons, a pair of lush twin peaks 2700-feet high, and you should take advantage of the palm-fringed anchorage with black sand beaches (Anse de Piton) nearby. If you can, anchor bow out and put a stern line to a palm tree, but make sure everything is secure, because The Pitons can generate some fierce wind gusts occasionally. Rodney Bay is another secure harbor, and a complete marina facility has shops, boutiques, and sprawling lawns.

A protected anchorage on St. Lucia shelters a pair of charter yachts in the lee of the towering mountain.

St. Vincent is not particularly popular with charterers since the locals, from boat boys to officials, can be irritatingly rude. The scenic sight on the island is the extensive Botanical Gardens.

THE GRENADINES

I know, I know, they're a part of the Windward Islands, but most of your charter brochures will list them separately, so I'm simply caving in to common usage.

The Grenadines, which stretch from St. Vincent to Grenada, are politically divided: St. Vincent owns those south to Mustique, while Grenada owns the remaining islands. With dozens of lovely anchorages, many charterers swear that a 10-day charter should be the minimum for this area. Ideally, a one-way charter allows you to explore the entire area at leisure, rather than retracing your steps, and some charter companies offer this option.

Because the harbor at Kingstown on St. Vincent is usually rough (and because the natives are often rude and unpleasant), most yachtsmen skip the

A charter yacht prepares to depart from the harbor at Grenada. (Courtesy of The Moorings.)

island and enter the Grenadines at Bequia (pronounced *beck*-wee).

Bequia's main harbor, Admiralty Bay, is usually filled with yachts, although it's interesting to look at the boats being built along the beachfront. You'll also be set upon by souvenir-sellers and musicians who arrive by boat and, if you go ashore, be sure to tip the youngsters who offer to guard your dinghy (no more than EC$5), or you'll find it cast adrift. On the east side of the island is Friendship Bay, a throwback to Moby Dick where the locals hunt whales in oar-powered longboats from January through March.

Mustique is best known for the jet set, including Princess Margaret, Raquel Welch and Mick Jagger, who own property on this island. The attraction is the snorkeling and, just off the north coast, is the wreck of the ocean liner *Antilles.* The only good anchorage on Mustique is Britannia Bay, which also has Basil's Bar for rum punches and fabulous lobster dinners.

Canouan Island is an overlooked prize, since it is usually missed by bareboaters intent on getting farther south. Charlestown Bay has an interesting settlement and, if you're a snorkeler, be sure to hire a guide to pilot your boat around to the east side, where the reefs are spectacular.

The Tobago Cays, however, are the jewels of the Grenadines, and the reason that many charterers return over and over again. Hidden from the Atlantic

St. George's is the capital of Grenada and one of the prettiest ports in the Caribbean.

behind World's End and Horseshoe Reefs, these four islands are probably the most photographed beaches and coves in the Caribbean. They are uninhabited and with easily navigated deep water channels, you can spend days wandering from one white beach to the next. At the height of the midwinter charter season, they can get busy, but there's always enough space for a few more yachts. The snorkeling on the reefs is fabulous and, on the beaches, you can easily find too many shells to keep. Your dinghy will get a real workout as everyone wants to go in different directions.

In good weather, you can anchor offshore at World's End Reef, a particularly appropriate name since there is no land between you and Africa or Europe.

Just west of the Cays is Mayreau, with the wreck of a World War I gunboat just offshore for divers to prowl and Dennis' Hideaway, the spot for delicious garlic-steamed lobster and conch fritters. Salt Whistle Bay is a protected and spectacular half-moon anchorage with a white sandy beach and shallow reefs for exploring on each side. Many cruising sailors say that Salt Whistle is the prettiest anchorage in the world. Don't be put off by the guidebooks which describe the reefs as dangerous. The reefs and rocks are plainly visible with ample room between them.

Union Island can be tricky, with a reef on the southern side, but Chatham Bay on the northwest side is protected and often deserted. Clifton Harbor is well protected even in bad weather, but watch out for the unmarked reef just offshore.

Carriacou is a leisurely island with boatbuilders and a hundred rum shops, with Tyrell Bay serving as a respite from the strong currents and sometimes rough seas found between Grenada and Carriacou, which also have the strange and craggy rocks called The Sisters and Kick 'Em Jenny.

Grenada is best known for the American "rescue mission" in the early 1980s, but it has settled down once again and is often called the most beautiful island in the Windwards. The best cruising is on the southwestern coast, although you may end up motorsailing because the mountains often block the breeze. You can spend a week exploring the coves and beaches.

The harbor at St. George's used to be one of the few places to see banana boats and trading schooners and, in addition to clearing in or out of the islands here, you can provision at the Foodland store right by the dinghy dock. The town is also pretty, with pastel houses rising up into the hillsides around the harbor. Prickly Bay at the south end has several charter bases, and is a good anchorage to start an exploration of the many southern bays. Grenada has earned its nickname as the Spice Island and, sailing close to shore after a rain squall, you can actually smell the nutmeg. If you want to get off your boat for a day, take a tour of the island, where everything grows profusely and there are some waterfalls in the mountains.

One last note about Caribbean chartering for sailors who like to cruise but miss the racing action they left at home. A growing number of regattas are being held throughout the Caribbean that not only permit but encourage bareboat charter entrants with separate classes.

The oldest and certainly most renowned is the previously mentioned Antigua Sailing Week every April, which has grown for over two decades. The pace at Antigua means an early afternoon race (which includes everything from maxi-boats to classic schooners), followed by beach activities such as inflatable races and wet T-shirt (or less) contests. In the evenings, the parties seem to go on endlessly, or at least that's how long the drums last.

Also in April are the Rolex Cup and the British Virgin Islands Regatta, both in BVI. While the waters are smoother, the racing is even more hard fought than at Antigua, particularly during the Rolex Cup when the trophies are watches. Other fast-growing events include the Heineken-sponsored regatta at St. Martin in March and the St. Barts Regatta in February.

Be sure to inform your charter company that you want to compete in one of these races, since some insurance policies exclude this sort of activity and you don't want to wind up uncovered. In addition, racing sails are generally not available, although some charter companies will allow you to bring your own spinnaker.

19

The Bahamas and North America

THE BAHAMAS

The Bahamian chain of islands stretches from Bimini, just 45 miles across the Gulf Stream from Miami, to the Turks, some 500-odd miles southwest. These 700 inhabited islands and 2400 uninhabited cays stretch the length of Cuba and end just north of Hispaniola.

Unlike the Caribbean islands, which are really undersea peaks that rise out of deep water, the Bahamas is a shallow plateau with a few low-lying cays. Where the Caribbean islands are usually lush and verdant, the Bahamas are sparse and rocky, but it is the water that makes these islands so attractive. With almost no runoff from the islands to muddy the water, it remains almost transparent and, as you sail along, you can look down at the white-pink sand and watch rainbow-colored fish dart around the coral heads. But though there are not the towering peaks of the Caribbean, you'll find more perfect sand beaches per mile than anywhere else.

One of the Bahamas is where Columbus actually discovered his new world, making landfall in 1492 on San Salvador. Pirates and privateers preyed from the many cays on merchant ships returning from South or Central America laden with treasure. Eventually many of the islands were settled by American Loyalists fleeing after the War of Independence, and many of their descendants are still there. In 1973, the Bahamas became an independent nation after three centuries as a British colony.

Today, the Bahamas rely heavily on tourist dollars, but charterers should be aware that the secluded cays and islets have also been used in recent years by drug smugglers who have shown little concern for lives or property. If you encounter suspicious activities, you should take extra precautions and probably find another anchorage. Be prepared to stop for inspections by Royal Bahamas Defence Force vessels as part of their battle against the smugglers.

Most chartering takes place in the Abacos and the Exumas, and there are major charter bases in both areas. Most of the Bahamas are served by airlines from the U.S. Unless you particularly enjoy pushing a shopping cart, we'd recommend taking the provisioning package from the charter company for Bahamas charters for two reasons. First, supermarkets are as rare as mountains in the Bahamas and, second, the prices for food can be double (or more) the cost in the U.S. Liquor, however, is cheap, with good rums about $5 per liter. In addition, there is often a 5% surcharge on credit card purchases. U.S. dollars are on a par with the Bahamian dollar, and are widely accepted.

It can be unnerving to sail with only a few feet of water under your keel but, after a day or two, you'll grow used to this thin-water cruising. Charts are generally reliable but, once you realize that Mother Nature has color-coded the shoals, you'll soon develop an eye for picking out the shallow spots. It's not hard to see the dark blotches of coral heads or rocks and, as the sand bottom shoals, it changes from a washed-out blue to shades of white which are the *uh-oh* areas.

While the Bahamian government has improved the navigational aids, bear in mind that this is not the United States and, when a bulb burns out, it may not get replaced for weeks. We arrived once in a squally norther at Marsh Harbour, but the expected beacon couldn't be seen. In between squalls, we used landmarks to follow the channel into the marina, but it was nerve-wracking because the dark sky made eyeball navigation nearly impossible. Later, having a calming gin and lime, we found that some of the regulars in the bar overlooking the channel had placed bets on whether we would make it, since the beacon had been turned off for several months!

When anchoring in some channels, the current can be quite strong, so you'll want to learn the Bahamas moor, which uses two anchors set as though they were to hold the bow and stern, but are both led from the bow. This allows the boat to pivot around the bow to the current or breeze without swinging through the anchorage.

Weather: Most seasons are pleasant, although the hurricane season runs from July to November. Most charters take place in the winter months, but the months from January to April can bring an occasional norther that blows 35+ knots and has heavy rain squalls. But a norther usually blows itself out quickly, leaving settled weather and light breezes behind. Starting in June, the summer month weather pattern brings light easterlies with frequent calms, as well as uncomfortable heat and humidity.

The Abacos

Lying at the northeastern edge of the Bahamas bank, the Abacos are protected by a long barrier reef, with a string of small cays on one side and Great Abaco Island on the other to form the Sea of Abaco. Among the small cays are islands such as Man-O-War Cay, New Plymouth and Hope Town, where the residents all seem to share the Loyalist names of Albury, Lowe, and Russell. The villages are also reminiscent of Cape Cod, with narrow streets and waterfront clapboard buildings. Some of these islands remain non-alcoholic, and all have a strong Christian ethic, so bear that in mind as you cruise. Conch (pronounced "conk") is a staple in the local diet, and you'll be offered everything from conch burgers to conch fritters.

Because there are so many distractions, not to mention the many doglegs in the channels, you should allow extra time even though the straight line distances are short. In a week, you can probably do the Sea of Abaco, seeing cays like those mentioned above plus Hope Town, Great Guana and Treasure Cay, but it would be better to have more time.

Marsh Harbour is the center of Abaco action, but it only has one stoplight and two good markets near the dinghy dock. Nearby Hope Town has perhaps the most photographed lighthouse in the world with its candy-striped tower.

A lone islet provides a sandy beach in the Abacos chain of the Bahamas for swimming in the warm waters.

Man-O-War Cay has a reputation for boatbuilding, and nearly everyone stops at Uncle Norman Albury's sail loft to buy souvenir duffle bags or canvas items.

Just north are Great Guana and Scotland Cays, both with outstanding snorkeling spots and, on the Atlantic side, the beaches are equally spectacular. At Green Turtle Cay is New Plymouth, an English-style village with pastel colored homes and the famous Blue Bee Bar at the south end of town with its walls papered with business cards of visiting sailors.

Grand Bahama and Bimini are usually not on the charterers route because of their distance and because they are congested with tourists and yachts from Florida.

The Exumas

Just over 100 miles south of the Abacos are the Exumas, which are a spectacularly pretty cruising area and Eleuthera is a good mid-point stopover for yachts sailing between the two island groups.

Mostly uninhabited, these cays create a smooth water buffer from the Atlantic. Highbourne Cay is usually the first stop, with provisions and evening calypso music as an enticement. At Allen's Cay, you can step back into prehistoric days as ancient iguanas lumber around hissing at you. Sampson's Cay is also appealing, and I can't think of Staniel Cay without my mouth watering for the tart key lime pie that you find there.

At Staniel, you can snorkel into nearby Thunderball Cave, where the James Bond film of the same name was shot, and which has been compared to the Blue Grotto at Capri, although it has more sealife and better lighting. Go during slack water, because the current is strong. Georgetown, on Great Exuma, is another charter base, and has a number of good bays close by.

NORTH AMERICA

The Florida Keys

The Keys conjure up images of Hemingway and Bogart, but these 800+ islands are the only tropical cruising to be found in North America. Nicknamed America's Out Islands and stretching for 130 miles from Key Largo to Key West, they offer the level of adventure you want, with choices ranging from large marinas to deserted channels surrounded by mangroves.

While the weather, vegetation and clear water are reminiscent of the Caribbean, there is an efficiency to cruising in your own country, with the Coast Guard, supermarkets, well-marked channels, and air-conditioned lodgings.

There are charter companies to be found in the Keys at Marathon as well as the Miami/Fort Lauderdale area and, depending upon your preferred style, you'll select from a wide variety of sail and powerboats. One caution, however: try to keep the draft of your charterboat under 4 feet or you'll be blocked from exploring some areas of the Keys.

Because the channels can be winding, narrow and shallow, the Keys are not ideal for sailboat charters. On the other hand, you may wish to charter a small powerboat for zipping out on day trips, using the many air-conditioned resorts for your overnight bases.

One of the treasures of the Florida Keys is the coral reef that stretches the length of these islands. The third largest living reef in the world, it has been declared a National Marine Sanctuary to prevent damage to this incredible ecosystem. More than one million visitors come to snorkel and dive on the reef, and there are mooring buoys to be used rather than anchors which damage the reef.

The Intracoastal Waterway is usually calmer than Hawk Channel (which runs inside the coral reef but otherwise open to the sea), and Plantation Yacht Harbor on Plantation Key has full facilities as well as a beach, which is a rarity in the Keys. The Intracoastal ends at Faro Blanco, whose harbor is marked by an old lighthouse and, after that point, you head outside to Hawk Channel unless your boat is shallow enough to poke around through the Keys.

Key West, at the tip of the Keys, has unfortunately turned into a major tourist trap, but you can still find pleasure in the old clapboard homes. During the season, you're well advised to radio ahead to reserve marina space since they fill up early.

If you have the time and inclination, heading offshore to explore the Marquesas Keys and the Dry Tortugas is worth the effort. The Marquesas are roughly 25 miles west of Key West, while the Dry Tortugas are another 50 miles. Choose your weather carefully, however, since the seas can become nasty if the weather turns bad.

On the way to the Marquesas, be sure to watch your chart carefully and keep your eyes open, as there are some coral heads when you near these islands. The harbor has just 3 feet of water, so larger boats need to anchor offshore.

The Dry Tortugas are far enough that they are rarely crowded, and Garden Key has Fort Jefferson, which was built during the Civil War. A nearby underwater trail is a fun diversion, and the rangers who staff the island can tell you where the best dive sites are to be found. Landing on Bush Key is prohibited because it is a wildlife sanctuary, but you can see huge numbers of birds during the summer nesting season.

Weather: The best time is from mid-January through May, although you can expect a few fronts to bring rain and cooler weather. June to September is hot (90° plus), humid and buggy, and the fall can be pleasant and uncrowded.

Chesapeake Bay

For more than 200 miles from mouth to headwaters, the Chesapeake Bay is one of the great American charter areas but it is also the homeport for an immense pleasure boat fleet, so you'll often find traffic jams in the busier marinas. Less a bay than a huge semi-protected waterway, the more than 3000 miles of shoreline are dotted with creeks and hidden anchorages, and the gently rolling scenery is not only beautiful but filled with history at every turning. While the numbers are arguable, there are about 230 harbors and 40 major rivers along the length of the Chesapeake.

A popular pastime is to explore the mazes of creeks and coves but don't try to cover too much ground: local boaters have spent dozens of summers without seeing it all. Sit back, enjoy the farms and villages sliding past, and remember that you can always return for more.

Don't be surprised if you run aground, however, since it's standard procedure for every skipper in the bay. Go slowly when you're not sure of the depth and you can usually back off easily from the mud or sand bottom.

Annapolis, of course, is a major boating center and, on pleasant weekends, the waters are literally covered with boats. You'll see fleets of training boats from the Naval Academy, and nearby Spa Creek is secluded and snug, with overhanging willows and fine homes. The in-water boatshows in October make this a less desirable time to visit, since there are no guest slips or hotel rooms available during this period.

Across the bay, you can explore the beautiful Chester River lined with impressive plantation homes, and Chestertown's elegant red brick Georgian buildings line the waterway.

St. Michael's on the Miles River has a superb maritime museum with guest moorings and a sleepy little town to explore, and you may see one of the famed Chesapeake log canoes out sailing with a tower of sail and the crew on hiking boards.

Tangier and Smith Islands provide a glimpse at fishing villages that haven't changed for a century, and the oddly Old English dialect spoken here traces back to the late 1600s.

Weather: The cruising season, depending on how much cold you can stand, generally ranges from mid-April through October, but the locals say the spring and fall are the best, with settled conditions and gentle breezes. Midsummer brings light to non-existent winds, humidity and heat waves, violent thunderstorms, and invasions of jellyfish. Because the Chesapeake stretches inland, you can't count on a sea breeze to provide natural air conditioning. Early October is my favorite time, with the leaves beginning to turn, the flights of birds heading south, and the sun still warm at midday.

The Northeast

From mid-Connecticut to Maine, there is superb sailing in areas with such famous names as Cape Cod and Narragansett Bay, or among islands such as Block and Nantucket. Along the shore are sailing centers such as Mystic and Newport, and there are charter boats to be found in every harbor.

Weather: The season runs roughly from May through October for the Northeast, and the summer winds are generally reliable, although fog can sometimes be a problem for days at a time.

Long Island Sound

Sometimes called the Dead Sea because of the notorious calms during the summer months, the sound is 90 miles long and 20 miles wide at the center. Because it is in the midst of the New York/Connecticut population center, this is an immensely popular sailing area in spite of the weather, which can be hot and humid in summer.

The entire shoreline is dotted with marinas, yacht clubs and marine facilities, so it's quite possible to spend an entire summer simply hopping from one cove to the next and, in fact, many Long Island sailors never take their boats offshore at all.

Maine

Maine is an area unto itself, known to old-timers as Down East (because it is downwind from Boston) and resembling Scandinavia in the rocky coves and islands found along the 200 miles of coastline. Although it is the same latitude as France, the Labrador Current sweeps past to ensure cold water year around and, when these waters meet the warm southwest winds, they turn Maine into a fog factory, with some areas averaging 75 foggy days a year.

Nevertheless, the beautiful scenery, sparse population, and crenellated coastline are an attraction for sailors. Only 250 miles in a straight line from border to border, there are literally thousands of miles of coastline when you include the coves, crannies, and more than 3000 islands, more than either French Polynesia or the Caribbean!

For the most part wild, rocky and forested, the scenery is dotted with clapboard buildings and myriad lighthouses.

Marinas outside the populated areas are few, but good anchorages are plentiful. Mount Desert is the largest of the many islands offshore, and the good harbors are often crowded in midsummer, although the creeks can often be empty.

Aside from the fog, navigation is straightforward, although you need to be prepared for up to 20 feet in tidal range, which can create fierce currents.

Weather: August is both the best cruising month and also the foggiest, and the short season lasts only from June through September.

Great Lakes

The largest body of fresh water in the world, the Great Lakes are truly a huge inland sea that can generate its own weather system. The more than 8000 miles of shoreline are often unspoiled, and several areas have become popular as charter cruising sites. All of the Great Lakes can turn stormy with little notice, and sailors make listening to the weather forecasts a regular part of their routine. In addition, you need a little humility because the lake levels change every year, and the charts may be a bit off in the depths, which gives you the opportunity to bump occasionally.

Remember that the U.S./Canadian border wanders through these lakes and, if you cross into Canada, you need to

This quiet anchorage in Mexico's Sea of Cortez has just a single charter yacht enjoying the clear water.

The islands offshore from Baja California in the Sea of Cortez are volcanic, with myriad coves to explore.

be sure that you report to Canadian immigration and customs promptly at the nearest town. Pets must have vaccination certificates, and Canadian law prohibits drinking except in licensed dining rooms and bars, or in your home. You are allowed to drink aboard your boat, but only when tied up or anchored and not underway.

The North Channel is a roughly 120 by 20 mile segment of Lake Huron along the Ontario shore of Canada and protected by Manitoulin Island from the lake itself. Most cruising sailors agree that the 40-mile stretch from Killarney at the east to Detour Passage in the west is the best portion. Sometimes described as a state of mind, the North Channel is, above all else, quiet and serene. With rocky beaches and forested islands, the coves are often deserted and the sense of solitude is a delight, particularly when you are within a day's sail of large cities. The coves are often closely spaced, but rarely more than 20 miles from a town or village that can provide a pump-out station for your holding tank or a fresh supply of beer. Little Current on Manitoulin Island has been called the social center of the North Channel. The storybook villages and spectacular rock formations, carved during the ice ages, are too numerous to mention and too numerous to include in a single charter, too.

The Apostle Islands at the western end of Lake Superior cover more than 1000 square miles off the coastline of Wisconsin, with primitive landscapes and deep protected anchorages on 22 islands, 21 of which are inhabited only by deer, eagles and loons. Known as the Apostle Islands National Lakeshore, strange geologic formations, worn by weather and glaciers, dot the area and hiking trails are found on most islands. Madeline Island has a quiet town much like a New England village. At the same latitude as Newfoundland, the water is chilly year around.

Georgian Bay, also on Lake Huron, has a multitude of rockbound islands along the east shore, while cliffs and fjord-like channels mark the west.

Weather: In general, June through September is the peak charter and cruising season for the Great Lakes. July is the busiest month because of the long days and warmer waters, but August has fewer mosquitoes, occasionally nippy evenings, and changeable weather. Normal wind patterns are westerlies that build in the afternoon before dying at night.

Baja California

Separated from the Pacific Ocean by the long arm of Baja California, the Sea of Cortez is one of the last great unspoiled cruising grounds. The beaches are still pristine and empty, the natives are actually friendly, and the sailing is marvelous. Until recently, the only way you could enjoy this area was if you were willing to voyage the 700+ miles down from California on your own boat, which limited the cognoscenti to cruising sailors jumping off for the South Seas, or the idle rich. Charter services now make this cruising solitude as close and convenient as the nearest airport.

La Paz is the capital of Baja California, a city of 50,000 souls mostly isolated from civilization except for the ferry to the Mexican mainland and jet flights from stateside. With complete provisioning and full marine services available, this harbor is a popular yachting port of call as well as the base for the new charter service.

Scattered both north and south of La Paz along the eastern shore of Baja are dozens of largely uninhabited islands. Espiritu Santo shimmers invitingly in the heat haze just 18 sea miles north of La Paz. Stretching eight miles in length, its craggy arms form a treasury of secluded coves and inlets, some with fresh water streams. Ashore, you might be treated to the sight of eagles feeding their young on a craggy volcanic cliff or find yourself being observed by timid desert animals. Rock hounds will delight in the geologic variety, and the truly indolent can contemplate a golden silence so pure it rings in the ears.

Snorkelers can scout the reefs or explore the famed oyster beds that once provided pearls for the crowns of Europe. The waters are swarming with fish, and even the most inept Walton may reel in a dorado or marlin.

Weather: November through May is the best cruising season, with warm days and soft nights. Be aware that in summer, both days and nights are hot and that fall can bring an occasional hurricane. A capricious local wind, the coromuel, can spring up suddenly, so keep your weather eye peeled.

Southern California

Sprawling from Santa Barbara at the north to San Diego huddled against the Mexican border, Southern California has one of the largest boating populations in the world. Marina del Rey, with more than 6000 boats, is the world's largest marina and Newport Harbor is much like Newport on the East Coast with its expensive waterfront homes and old money atmosphere.

In between are literally hundreds of marinas, which is somewhat of a surprise because cruising destinations (other than going to another marina) are somewhat limited.

Certainly the most popular destination is Catalina Island which, as the song says, is "26 miles across the sea." Avalon is the only village on the island, but Two Harbors is a smaller outpost located at a narrow isthmus near the west end of the island. Many of the coves are privately leased to yacht clubs, but there are still open anchorages in addition to the mooring buoys provided at Avalon and Two Harbors, although your chances of finding an empty buoy after breakfast on a summer Saturday aren't worth mentioning.

The Long Beach/Los Angeles Harbor, tucked behind a protective breakwater, is a mini-cruising area by itself. Further south, Newport Harbor has Balboa Island in mid-channel, and is literally wall-to-wall yachts, although transient moorings are available.

San Diego has an immense harbor that can take a day to sail to one end and back, and Mission Bay nearby is a huge manmade water playground with areas set aside for sailing, waterskiing, and swimming.

Weather: The boating season is year around, with the summer being the most stable and the warmest, of course. The westerly seabreeze is reliable, although an occasional Santa Ana, a hot offshore breeze, can whistle down the canyons in the fall bringing 40-knot blasts suddenly.

Sacramento Delta

The California Delta is always a surprise to sailors unfamiliar with the area. San Francisco, just 60-odd miles away, is renowned for the icy gales that blow through the Golden Gate, but the Delta is another world, one that Northern Californians use to balance out their rugged coastal waters.

Many visitors expect to see the undercivilized world and muddy backwaters of a Huck Finn story, but the sight of huge ocean-going freighters heading up river, or the glimpse of a maxi-ocean racing yacht nestled behind an island quickly changes that impression.

With more than 1000 miles of navigable waterways, the Delta is a vast network supplied by three rivers: the San Joaquin, Sacramento and Mokelumne. Both Sacramento and Stockton are deepwater ports served by large ships, but it's the backwaters that attract the yachting crowd and that provide the basis for a booming houseboat charter business.

The Delta was once just lowland marsh, but a vast reclamation project was started in the mid-1800s, using Chinese labor from the transcontinental railroad to build levees and turn river bottoms into fertile farmlands. Where paddlewheel steamers once raced with mail and passengers, ski boats zip up and down the wide rivers, marlin-equipped sportfishers are tied to trees on the banks, and sailboats drift along in the gentle breezes. The mail is delivered by a postman in an outboard skiff, law and order is upheld by sheriffs in a flotilla of runabouts, and children use dinghies to catch the school bus.

Every area of the Delta has a personality of its own, and you can pick your spot by your mood. The Meadows, probably the best known area, and Lost Slough, both boast overhanging trees with branches trailing in the water, cool green glades, and silence that is almost overwhelming. Yet you're only a few minutes by runabout from several Delta hotspots where you can party late into the night. The settlement of Locke, built by and for the Chinese labor force, is almost a ghost town, with weathered clapboard buildings, creaky boardwalks, and fading paint marking a once-thriving playhouse.

If you want to keep moving, you can cruise along levees where, as in Holland, you're far above the farms as brightly colored crop dusters dart back and forth. If you'd rather sprawl in the cockpit with a cold beer and a lurid novel, you need only to find a convenient tree trunk and hitch up.

A sailboat is moored to the levee bank on the Sacramento Delta inland of San Francisco, with a runabout tied nearby for afternoon waterskiing.

Weather: The climate is one of the drawing cards for the Delta, with hot summer afternoons and balmy evenings. Spring and fall are usually bright with cool evenings, while winter is pleasant, although the fogs sometimes rival London's best.

Pacific Northwest and Canada

Certainly the most popular charter area in the Western United States is the San Juan Island chain, some 60 nautical miles north of Seattle. Charter boat fleets abound in Anacortes, which is just a few miles away on the mainland. If the San Juans are your cruising destination, try to pick up your boat nearby. I once chartered a Seattle-based boat and, by the time I had checked out the boat, passed through two locks and headed north up Puget Sound, I'd lost an entire day, as well as another one at the end of the charter for the return trip.

With more than 200 rocky islands (750 if you count the small ones at low tide) and a dozen state parks left undisturbed, the forests and small villages are reminiscent of Maine. A good chartering area for beginners, the waters are reasonably protected even in storms off the Pacific. Friday Harbor, on San Juan Island, is the social and political center of the area, with a pleasant municipal marina and a one-street town lined with shops and restaurants. If you

Friday Harbor is the heart of the San Juan Islands, with a well-equipped marina and a pleasant village to attract charter crews.

Children play on rocks worn by the ice age in Sucia Island's Fossil Bay in the heart of the San Juan Islands.

don't want that much civilization, you can leave the madding crowd behind and pick from the isolated outer islands, such as Stuart, with Reid and Prevost Harbors lying opposite each other, or Sucia Island, where Fossil Bay shows the ice age evolution of this island chain through embedded fossils and gouged rock. Roche Harbor, on the opposite side of San Juan Island, has a Victorian-era hotel where Teddy Roosevelt once stayed, and the marina has a flag-lowering ceremony every evening followed by a weather forecast that takes delight in listing other less fortunate cities across the nation.

Puget Sound, stretching for 75 miles from the tip of the Olympic Peninsula past Seattle and Tacoma to the myriad inlets and creeks at the southern end, is another popular cruising area, also dotted with small towns, marinas, and anchorages.

North of the U.S./Canadian border are equally interesting charter areas, and the Gulf Islands are really just a continuation of the San Juans under Canadian jurisdiction, although they tend to be more rocky than their southern kin.

Further north, the Strait of Georgia forms an inland waterway under the protective bulk of Vancouver Island. Probably the most visited site for charterers is Princess Louisa Inlet, some 40 miles up Jervis Inlet and past Malibu Rapids, where you have to wait for slack water to transit the tidal rapids. Once inside, however, the scenery is stunning, with 5000-foot cliffs towering over the five-mile-long inlet, and Chatterbox Falls tumbling 120 feet down into the saltwater. Below the surface, the fjord is more than 1000-foot deep. At dusk, you may see a bear strolling along the shore looking for dinner, and the smell of the pine forest lingers on the quiet air.

Given enough time, you can explore much of the coast of British Columbia, and Penmar Charters offers a yearly circumnavigation of Vancouver Island as a flotilla effort with crews joining and leaving at various points along the way.

You can even find charter activity in Alaska, with Juneau being close to Glacier Bay National Park, the Tracy Arm-Fords Wilderness Area, and the Admiralty Island National Monument. A chain of high islands protects the Alaskan waterways, but the strong currents and large tidal range mean this is an area for experienced skippers only.

Weather: Even in summer, the area is marked by rain and the winds are predominately light. The peak cruising season is the summer, of course, from June through September, and the San Juans can be crowded from both visiting yachtsmen and tourists arriving by ferry. I prefer the shoulder seasons of May and early October when the islands are once again quiet and the weather is pleasant, although often nippy in the evenings.

20

Europe

For most Americans, chartering in Europe means the Mediterranean, that cauldron of ancient and modern culture that ranges from Spain's orange groves past the jet-set playgrounds of France, Monaco and Italy to the birthplace of civilization, Greece. Included are seas with romantic names: Tyrrhenian, Ionian, Aegean, Adriatic, as well as a handful of major islands such as Malta, Sardinia and Mallorca. New chartering areas have developed along the Turkish coast.

The flip side of this sun-drenched Europe is the dramatic scenery and challenging sailing to be found in Northern Europe on the Baltic and North Seas as well as parts of the Atlantic. From Helsinki, Finland, on the east to the wild Hebrides of Scotland on the west, there is another world to explore with literally thousands of islands, the fjords of Scandinavia and the lochs of Scotland providing grand landfalls and spectacular cruising.

GREECE

Greece is certainly the most popular charter area in Europe, and thus worthy of a separate section. You can't sail in Greece without thinking often of Homer and, though I've never seen his wine dark seas, the shades of pale to dark blue are a stunning substitute. Everywhere you look, there are ancient ruins and history to be absorbed, but there is beauty as well. The villages, pouring down the hillsides to the tiny harbors like waterfalls of red tile roofs and

Showing the influence of a Moorish past, this Greek harbor has pure Greek caiques at the quay.

whitewash, are a contrast to the hillsides covered with olive trees, flashing silvery leaves in the sun. In the evenings, you can sit in your cockpit and listen to the soft sounds of bouzouki music drifting from the local tavernas.

Greece is a delight for charter sailors, because the distances are relatively short between harbors, the navigation is purely by eyeball and, aside from the strong northeasterly meltemi, the weather is as stable as in the Caribbean. The only real test for North American sailors is to learn how to Med-moor stern-to the quays, which can prove a challenge in a crowded harbor with a crosswind. But, once settled in, the mooring is secure, doesn't require a dinghy to get ashore, and most crews pick up the technique easily.

The most popular cruising areas are the Saronic and Argolic gulfs which are close to the charter bases at Piraeus as well as the gateway city of Athens. The popular islands of Aegina, Póros, Hydra and Spetsai form a natural path leading to the Argolic Gulf. Because the distances are relatively short (25 miles or less), there is time for leisurely sightseeing in the mornings before the breeze comes up, and in the afternoons after arriving in a new harbor.

The village of Perdica on Aegina is the first stop for most yachts since it is

The harbor of the Greek island of Hydra sprawls upwards from the quay, which is dotted with traditional fishing craft.

just 15 miles from Piraeus (the seaport of Athens), and the island is noted for pistachio nuts, which you can buy fresh roasted from street vendors.

Póros, with more than 30,000 lemon trees, has great coves for a lunch stop and swim on the way to Hydra, which is a popular port for charterers. With the town built like an amphitheater on the slopes around the harbor, you can moor within feet of the outdoor tavernas that line the quay, but arrive early because the harbor fills up quickly.

Spetsai is forested with olive, cypress and lemon trees that soften the rugged Greek terrain, and was featured in John Fowles' novel *The Magus.* No private automobiles are allowed on the island, and all transportation is either by taxi or horse-drawn carriage along streets lined with brilliantly white buildings.

The Northern Sporades Islands on the eastern side of Greece are another popular area, with some of the prettiest islands in the entire Mediterranean. Often thickly wooded, the islands are a contrast to those in the Saronic Gulf. Skiathos with its charter base, Skópelos, memorable for a pretty village rising steeply above the harbor, and Skyros, which has a fortified village, are the best known.

The Dodecanese Islands are Greek but closer to Turkey and similar in scenery. Kos is a charter base, dominated by a Crusader castle and known as the birthplace of Hippocrates, the father of modern medicine. Kálymnos is the sponge fishing capital of the world, Leros has spectacular anchorages and Pátmos has the monastery of St. John looming over the whitewashed houses.

The Ionian Sea along the west coast of Greece has several charter bases for exploring a sea of islands. Lefkas is blanketed with wild flowers in the spring, and there are dozens of pretty coves to explore, while Meganisi, Kálamos and the mainland coast near Astakos are equally inviting. Of all the areas, the Ionian has the least number of ancient ruins, however.

At every island, you can find wonderful food, including fresh tomatoes, olives, oranges, strawberries and melons, plus the local yogurts, feta cheese, and fluffy pastries. No matter how well you stocked your charter boat, you'll end up buying fresh island bread just because of the smells wafting from the bakeries.

Greek time needs to be mentioned, since it is different from other European countries. Shops open early in the mornings and stay open late into the evening, but most residents take a lengthy midday nap. Dinner is late, with some restaurants not serving until after 9 pm. English is widely spoken, and both travelers checks and major credit cards are generally accepted throughout the Greek islands.

Weather: The summers are hot and have the strong meltemi winds from late June to early September. My favorite season is from mid-April to mid-May, when the temperatures range from 60° to 80°, the winds are lighter but reliable, the crowds of tourists haven't arrived for the summer season, and mooring space is available. In the spring, the Aegean is still in bloom with flowers, green hills and water is plentiful. The after-summer season runs from mid-September to the end of October with similar conditions, but I've found that, after the tourist crush of summer, the local citizenry is weary rather than outgoing as they are before the summer.

MEDITERRANEAN

Stretching 2300 miles from Gibraltar to the shores of Lebanon and Israel, the Med is a vast and tideless sea, warmed by the hot lands of North Africa and by the southern shores of Europe. The North African and Middle Eastern coast is generally inhospitable, both in cruising facilities and because of the general civil unrest that affects the region.

The northern shore, however, is just the opposite and provides some superb cruising for charterers, including Greece, which we've already covered separately since it is such a popular destination. The Spanish coast is pretty but undeveloped for chartering, but everything changes at the French border. The Riviera has two faces, with low hills and sandy beaches from Cap Roux to Nice, and the distinctive reddish mountains from Nice to the Italian border, with cliffs to the water's edge and numerous harbors.

There are a number of charter companies operating along the Riviera, but

A charter yacht is anchored off Mallorca while the crew swims idly in the clear waters.

One of the best known destinations on the French Riviera, St. Tropez is lined with cafes and Med-moored yachts.

A lone charter yacht enjoys a private anchorage along the Costa Smeralda of Sardinia.

Porto Cervo, the heart of jet-set Costa Smeralda on the Italian island of Sardinia, attracts mega-yachts as well as charterers.

this is a different type of chartering which caters to those who prefer their pleasures ashore rather than at sea. With light breezes throughout the summer, most charterers simply cruise from port to port, mooring Med-style and going ashore to sample the gastronomic and shopping pleasures of ports such as St. Tropez, Antibes, Cannes and Portofino.

Corsica, lying south of Genoa, is nevertheless French and quite beautiful, with 9000-foot mountains, palm-lined beaches and ancient buildings. The water is clear and warm, with good sailing breezes, although you need to watch for navigation hazards like underwater rocks. The island has several charter companies, some of which have two bases for one-way charters, and it's an easy sail to the Costa Smeralda jet-set playgrounds on Sardinia or to Elba, which has many lovely coves and anchorages.

Weather: The cruising season for the Riviera is long by most charter standards, ranging from April through the end of October, but I would avoid August like the plague, since most of Europe takes their vacation at that time. In fact, summer tourist traffic into towns like Portofino can be so bad that it takes several hours to travel a single mile, so I'd be wary of June through August in general.

TURKEY

At the eastern end of the Med lies Turkey, which is a relatively recent addition to the charter world. The pine-covered mountains and occasional waterfalls are a pleasant change from the dry and rocky islands in the Med, but the turquoise seas and sheltered bays are the real drawing cards.

The Aegean coast and the Mediterranean shores are the most popular, since the Black Sea along northern Turkey has many restricted areas. The western and southern coastline is dotted by a multitude of pretty bays, beaches and harbors, as well as incredible historical and archaeological sites worthy of exploration.

The foods of Turkey blend Asia and Europe, with shish kebabs, incredible fresh vegetables, and good wines. Be wary of raki, an aniseed aperitif which is known locally as *lion's milk* with good reason. Carpet shops are found under awnings, and you will barter for your Persian rug over a cup of tea in a most civilized manner. Provisions and water are generally available, marinas are found in the larger cities, and the fresh produce markets are exceptional throughout Turkey.

Bodrum is a charter base as well as the yachting capital of Asia Minor, and has a magnificent Knights of Rhodes fortress dating to the 1400s, as does the other charter base of Marmaris (not to be confused with the Sea of Marmaris), just 30 miles from Rhodes with a sixteenth century fortress overlooking the city. Between Marmaris and Antalya are a number of delights: the ruins of Xanthus with its long beach, the port towns of Kas and Kalkan, Kekova with dozens of islets and a sunken Lycian city to snorkel, and Antalya, close to the great sites of Perge and Side. Fethiye, near the southern tip, lies on a bay filled with lovely islands and gleaming white sand beaches, overlooked by the rock tombs of former kings.

Weather: The Turkish summers are hot (July and August as high as 100°) and crowded, and the Aegean shore is affected by the meltemi from May through September, while the southern coastline has light breezes and calm nights. Thunderstorms are most frequent in spring and autumn. In general, the cruising season is from early April through October, with experienced charterers picking October as the best month.

WESTERN EUROPE

While the Mediterranean coast of France is the more famous, the best sailing is certainly along the Brittany coast, which also has a number of charter bases. Morbihan (Breton for little sea) has 50 mostly uninhabited islands with white sand beaches, good anchorages, and a warm, sunny climate. There are creeks and villages to explore, as well as some lovely old towns like Vannes, with its thirteenth century cathedral and Auray with its gabled houses. Again, you have to be prepared for an extreme tidal range as well as river-like currents. You can even sail up the River Vilaine to the city of Redon, passing wonderful creeks for overnight mooring as well as towns and villages to explore.

The Netherlands is more water than land, and most of it is reclaimed from the sea by technology and tenacity. The Ijsselmeer (pronounced ice-el-mir) was created in 1932 when the Zuiderzee was cut off from the North Sea by massive dikes and, fed by rivers, it is now the largest fresh water lake in Europe as well as a popular charter cruising area. With steady 15-20 knot breezes and short distances between the marinas and villages, it is a pleasant area for novices and experts alike.

Volendam is touristy but pretty, with colorful houses along the water, while Muiden has an excellent marina and a massive castle, Muiderslot, that dates to 1280. Hoorn is a charming shipping town, and Makkum is notable for beautiful pottery that uses more colors than the traditional Delft blue. You can even sail up the Amstel River to the edge of Amsterdam if you want a taste of cosmopolitan life.

Aside from the Ijsselmeer, the Waddenzee is a less populated area on the North Sea coast, and Zeeland is an area of islands and inlets bordering Belgium.

Weather: Throughout most of Western Europe, the sailing season runs from May through September. The climate is temperate, with temperatures rarely above 65° in summer, and rainfall is frequent year around.

THE BRITISH ISLES

England, Wales, Scotland and Ireland offer an almost endless variety of chartering possibilities, as well as something for every level of skill and

Sailing offshore in Scotland is challenging, since there are few good harbors like this one at Portree on the Isle of Skye.

pocketbook. Changeable weather, strong tidal currents, and rain are a part of the boating life throughout the British Isles.

Scotland

When I tell people that one of my favorite charter cruising areas is Scotland, they always look at me oddly, as though white sand beaches, balmy weather and bathing suits are a prerequisite for any interesting sail.

Scotland is often windy and wet, but it is also purple heather and yellow gorse turning the hillsides into brilliant color, and it is challenging sailing for the experienced crew. Though there are many charter companies in both sail and power, few North Americans take advantage of this wild country.

The Hebrides, where Gaelic is the native tongue, provide spectacular Highlands scenery, with towering mountains and pristine villages on protected harbors. On the negative side, this is the Atlantic Ocean and storms are not a rarity, while the tides can be as much as 19 feet in some areas. Currents sweep between the islands, so your navigation must be accurate, but you can find inside passages to most of the interesting areas. Oban is a popular charter base, from which you can easily sail to the islands of Skye, Mull, Eigg and Rhum. The main harbor on Skye is

Urquhart Castle on Scotland's Loch Ness provides a quiet anchorage, although you aren't guaranteed a sighting of Nessie.

Portree, with a row of brightly painted houses lining the main quay, but there are numerous good anchorages on most of the islands. While the season generally ranges from late April to the end of September, I think the best time is in May and June, when the weather seems to be more settled.

One of my most interesting cruises took place inside Scotland, when I chartered a powerboat on the Caledonian Canal, which cuts through the heart of Scotland in a chain of locks that connect the lochs, including the fabled Loch Ness. No, we didn't see Nessie, but we did anchor in the lee of a ruined castle and we locked right through the center of a town, where we could shop while waiting for the water to rise.

The English Channel

The most popular charter area in England is on the Solent, a 20 mile stretch of the English Channel bounded by the Isle of Wight. From the hundreds of marinas in that area, you can explore the creeks and harbors along the English coast, going as far as Devon and Cornwall where the scenery is spectacular. You can also sail to France (Cherbourg is just 65 miles from the Isle of Wight) or, in a long week, you can explore the Channel Islands.

Channel Islands

A part of the United Kingdom, although with their own parliament and tax system, the five major Channel Islands are just 85 miles from the Solent, but this is for the experienced sailor since there is an extreme tidal range as well as currents as high as 10 knots with overfalls in the Alderney Race area. This area is one of the most hazardous in Europe, with swirling currents, hidden rocks and often changeable weather. But the islands such as Jersey and Guernsey are delightful, and Sark is a tiny kingdom that permits no cars and has three tiny harbors for access to the beautiful countryside.

The French coast of Brittany and Normandy is equally challenging, with harbors that dry out at low tide, but there are also many islands, uncrowded beaches, and a sunny climate that seems closer to the Riviera than the English Channel.

Weather: English sailing is just what you might expect—a little of everything. Pack your sweaters and foul-weather gear along with your suntan cream because even in mid-summer, you can have both bright sun and pouring rain just hours apart. Good weather forecasts are available for the British Isles, and you should make a point of listening religiously.

Ireland

Another area often overlooked by North American charterers, Ireland has some superb sailing along the south and southwest coasts. Make no mistake: there are open sea passages that can test your skills and your stomach, but these are mercifully short and lie between protected sailing areas with good harbors.

Crosshaven is close to the international entry at Shannon, and the Royal Cork Yacht Club is the oldest in the world. From there, you can sail as far as Bantry Bay, exploring harbors like Oysterhaven with its emerald green hillsides or Kinsale, a yachting center lined by beautiful Georgian homes. Castle Haven has a village with nearly vertical streets, and the beautiful harbor at Adrigold is protected by well-marked shoals. In between, you'll find numerous villages where you can stay in marinas while you sample the Guinness in the local pub, or you might choose secluded inlets (beware of those that dry out!) for solitude. Charterers can even sail out to Fastnet Rock, but watch your weather because it was a sudden gale that brought carnage to the experienced fleet in the 1979 Fastnet Race.

Weather: Irish weather is, like the people, temperamental. Though the Gulf Stream flows along the coast, the water is cold even in mid-summer, and the air temperature rarely reaches 80° even during the season from May through September.

SCANDINAVIA

From Finland on the east to Norway on the west, the whole of Scandinavia is a smorgåsbord of delights, offering generally protected cruising grounds (especially in the areas where charter fleets are based), friendly people, often uncrowded anchorages and, though at a higher latitude, a warmer and drier climate than Britain.

Mooring in Scandinavia is the reverse of the Mediterranean practice where you back into the quay with a bow anchor out. Instead, northern sailors drop a stern anchor and then tie the bow to a tree or rock. You'll often see iron rings pounded into the rocks by the local sailing clubs for use on a first-come, first-served basis (unless marked private), and you'll know you've found a good anchorage.

Finland's biggest archipelago is off Turku in the southwest, with hundreds of islands in a 50-mile arc. To the east in the Gulf of Bothnia are the Åland Islands where more than 6500 islands lie between Finland and Sweden. Turku is a major base for charter companies, while Hangö is a popular Finnish sailing resort. Because of the high latitude (most of the country is above 60°N, or higher than Anchorage, Alaska), the sailing season lasts from mid-June to mid-August, although there is almost perpetual daylight during those months. Even in summer, the forested islands are usually deserted.

Sweden's sun coast is from Stockholm south about 120 miles along the Baltic sea coast roughly to Västervik, with sheltered sailing in the lee of the mainland. The Swedish coast has literally thousands of islands and in this area are three spectacular archipelagos. Starting at the north is the Stockholm archipelago, which is really three distinct chains of islands with a reported 24,000 islets within an easy sail of the capital. Further south are St. Anna's and Grynt, which offer an infinite choice of harbors and coves.

The islands are rocky remnants of the ice age glaciers, and Swedish sailors often moor by using a stern anchor and a line tied from the bow to shore, or you can round moor as they call swinging on a single anchor in mid-harbor. The Swedes respect privacy and solitude, so you'll find the anchorages quiet and fairly empty. Marinas are infrequent and there are few restaurants ashore, so plan to be self-sufficient once you leave the charter base. Liquor, by the way, is available only from state-owned stores, so stock up before you depart.

Navigation in Sweden (as in all of Scandinavia) is easy, with excellent charts and buoyage systems but, because the islands are gardens of rocks, it's easy to get disoriented. Keep track of your position on the chart or you'll wind up wondering where you are in the maze. One pleasant attribute to the area is zero degree of magnetic variation, which simplifies your chartwork.

Denmark consists mostly of islands, and the waters are well-protected from North Sea storms. Distances are short between the many harbors and coves, so you can easily find yourself stopping several times in a single day to explore. Denmark is lower and less mountainous that Sweden or Finland, and the island scenery consists of rolling hills and quaint villages.

The most popular cruising areas are the islands south of the main islands of

Norway's fjords are often calm, but their depth sometimes makes anchoring a problem.

Fyn and Sjaelland, while the northern end of Jutland shelters the waters of Limfjord, which connects the North Sea to the Kattegat. There are a multitude of marinas and yacht harbors, so many charterers choose to pick up moorings or transient docks every night, leaving their exploration of empty coves to the daytime. The Danish Yachting Association has mooring buoys (marked DS) in 23 harbors in Limfjord, and south of Fyn and Sjaelland, which can be used by visiting sailors for 24 hours with no charge.

Norway is probably the wildest of the Scandinavian cruising grounds, with deep fjords and sheltered islands. There are several charter bases on the southern and western coasts for both power and sailboats, and the rugged scenery is spectacular. There are few marinas, but every village has mooring space available for transient boats, whether they are fishing vessels or charter boats.

Weather: At 55°-60°N, the summers are short and brisk, ranging from May through September in Denmark and Sweden to June-August in Norway and Finland. The long days fade into a half-light from midnight to a 4 a.m. dawn in Finland and Norway, so you have plenty of time to sail in daylight. Temperatures can range into the 70s during the days, although you'd be well advised to pack as many sweaters and jackets as you do bathing suits and shorts, because the conditions are changeable. Winds are generally light to moderate, although you can expect gusts near the valleys in Norway and Finland.

21

The South Pacific and Asia

After Nordhoff and Hall wrote of *Bounty*'s landfall at Tahiti, generations of armchair sailors have dreamed of the scent of the South Pacific. The jumbo jet and the charter yacht have brought this area into the range of every sailor, who can now smell the frangipani on a warm tradewind.

TAHITI

Known officially as the Society Islands, this French archipelago lies halfway between Australia and California, and the primary charter grounds are the Leeward Islands (Iles Sous le Vent) at the northern end of the island chain. For most armchair cruisers, the names of Bora Bora, Huahine, and Raiatea conjure up images of coco palms swaying over clear blue water and jagged volcanic peaks thrusting into vivid South Pacific sunsets. Best of all, it's true. The Society Islands of French Polynesia are the stuff of dreams.

Four major islands comprise the chartering area: Raiatea, Tahaa, Bora Bora and Huahine. While Tahaa and Raiatea share the same boundary reef, the other two islands are roughly a half day's sail away. Once inside the protective reefs (entrances are well marked), you can sail for hours in the smooth waters past the jagged volcanic mountains and lush green valleys. Anchorages are plentiful both on the islands themselves, as well as on the motus, tiny islets on the barrier reef, and there's no shortage of either lunch stops for swimming on the white sand beaches or protected harbors for stress-free overnighting.

On a seven-day charter, you'll have to make some tough decisions since there is too much to be seen in such a short time. Bora Bora, of course, is a must, if only to sail through the pass and see the magnificent peaks wreathed in clouds. Huahine, particularly the southern end, is unspoiled, as are the southern and northern areas of both Raiatea and Tahaa.

Raiatea would be enough for a week's vacation alone, and some charterers never depart from the Raiatea/Tahaa reef, spending their days exploring the numerous deep fjords and the motus. Uturoa, the main town in the Leewards, offers a taste of French Polynesia without the jaded and grimy feel of Papeete, the capital and main city in Tahiti which is now overrun by tourists. By contrast, Uturoa has friendly people and a leisurely pace still unaffected by the dozens of jumbo jets that descend into Tahiti. Uturoa also has an incredible fresh produce market and the volcanic soil produces superb fruit, including a sweet pineapple not to be missed.

Bora Bora, with two extinct volcanoes rising from a cobalt sea, is one of the world's most recognizable landfalls and was the inspiration for the mythical Bali Hai in *South Pacific*. Because of that attraction, it is dotted with tourist hotels and is a typical Club Med playground, but you can still find pleasant anchorages and superb snorkeling away from the shoreside disco atmosphere. Be sure to get a radio check on the single pass through the reef before heading for Bora Bora, however, because it is sometimes closed by breaking seas.

Raiatea is known as the sacred one to Polynesians. You won't be the only ones to set sail from this largest island in the Leeward chain, though, since every great Polynesian sea voyage began from a marae, or temple, at Opoa on this island, including the migrations to Hawaii and New Zealand.

Huahine is the garden island, steadfastly cultivating crops rather than tourists, so it remains much as Captain Cook might have seen it. The usual first stop on Huahine is off the village of Fare, but the lagoon at Baie d'Avea at the south end of the island is a pretty anchorage with a good sand bottom and an astounding reef filled with brilliantly colored, and fearless, tropical fish. (When packing for the charter, include a bottle of hydrogen peroxide or Betadine antiseptic to treat any coral cuts, which will quickly become infected otherwise.) Port Bourayne at mid-island is startling because, once through the narrow entrance, it is as though you have entered a Scottish loch.

From Huahine, you can sail to Tahaa for lunch at the Hibiscus Hotel, where you'll be greeted by the immense pet pig, Lala. The motus at the north end of Tahaa provide good anchorages and Motu Diego has the François restaurant, which serves truly gourmet (but expensive) food at a bungalow-getaway owned by a charming French/Swiss couple.

While the trips between the major islands involve open sea crossings, the steady 15-20 knot tradewinds provide

Off the shore of Tahaa in French Polynesia, this crew sails in company with a school of dolphins who love to play in the bow waves of charter yachts.

reasonably predictable breezes for much of the year. You need to remember that all of Polynesia uses the European IALA-A buoyage system with red to port (red-to-red returning) and, inside the reefs, a hybrid system marks the lagoons by land or reef side, but all buoys are well maintained. Navigation is "sail by colors," with dark blue being deep, light blue or brown being thin, and white (either transparent or foamy) water being never-never land. All of the charter boats are equipped with anchor windlasses, a necessity since you will often be anchoring in water as deep as 100 feet in the island fjords. Because of the dangers of navigating at night, the charter companies suggest that you be anchored by 5:30 pm, and leave for other islands before 9:30 am to make sure you arrive early.

French Polynesia has acquired a well-deserved reputation for being expensive, so you should plan to dine aboard regularly and save restaurants for special occasions. A bottle of Hinano, a local beer, is $3-4 at a bar, a decent French wine is $12-16 at a restaurant, and a hamburger with fries can be $10. Be sure to bring enough sunblock, film and other necessities, because they are pricey ashore. On the other hand, it's hard to leave a village without a baguette of French bread (the smell wafts from

Anchored off a motu in French Polynesia, this trio of charter yachts is enjoying typically perfect tradewinds and warm sun.

the bakeries), a plastic jug of pleasant vin ordinaire, or a cone of homemade coconut ice cream.

Chartering in the Leewards is almost more accessible than the Caribbean, particularly from the West Coast where the non-stop flights take just 8 hours, and Raiatea is a quick shuttle of 45 minutes farther. Now is the time to go, however, because hotels are abuilding and there is a real fear that the Leeward Islands will soon become Waikiki South.

Weather: The charter high season is from June through September, which is winter below the equator, when the tradewinds blow steadily from the southeast. The months from November through April are the wet season, with high humidity, occasional rain, warm temperatures and light breezes. The dry season is from May through October, with lower humidity and steady tradewinds. Temperatures average 79°F, ranging to the 90s in the wet season and mid-80s in the dry.

TONGA

Tonga is a land that time forgot, although it is called "the land where time begins" because it lies on the International Dateline where each new day starts. But Tonga also lives up to the nickname The Friendly Islands, applied when Captain James Cook first visited these gorgeous islands in the late 1700s. Time does seem to stand still and life proceeds at a much more sedate pace in Tonga.

The last of the Polynesian kingdoms, Tonga has the longest unbroken monarchy in the world. Lying between 15° and 23.5° S, Tonga consists of three distinct archipelagoes, but it is Vava'u, the northernmost chain, that is the charter area. Because of a string of islands and reefs that shelter the islands from the wind and seas of the open Pacific, the Vava'u group is essentially an island-studded lake, with conditions similar to those in the Virgin Islands. The breezes are the steady tradewinds that sweep the Pacific, and the water is warm and remarkably clear.

Best of all, there are more than 50 anchorages that one charter company terms world class, and all are spectacularly beautiful and close together, so you can explore several in a day.

Because Tonga has remained off the beaten path for so many centuries, it hasn't been civilized, so the Tongans remain proud, gracious and gentle. Tipping is not permitted because good service is considered normal. The Sabbath remains as a day of rest, and no Tongan can be found swimming, fishing, playing games and certainly not working. In fact, a check signed on a Sunday is not valid. By the same token, the dress code ashore remains conservative, and men are expected to wear shirts in public, while women should leave their bikinis to the privacy of the boat or an uninhabited islet.

Neiafu is the biggest town in the Vava'u chain, and the base of charter operations. The eastern islands are low and surrounded by the protective reefs, while the western islands rise from deep water and are volcanic remains. Maninita is as far south as most charterers venture, but it is a hauntingly beautiful island where you can anchor off a talcum-soft beach and row ashore. The big leafed puleo trees turn the interior into a cool, green glade that silences even the noise of the surf, and you can easily walk across to the ocean beaches on the opposite side.

Hunga Lagoon is nearly landlocked, and you can sail west from Hunga if you want to try your hand at deepsea game fishing for tuna, dorado and the occasional sailfish, but be sure to request fishing gear from the charter company. Just south is Foeata, a pretty lunch anchorage with excellent snorkeling, as is Mounu.

One surprise to charterers are the sea caves of Tonga, which you are encouraged to explore. Swallows Cave is on the northern tip of Kapa Iskand, and you should row into the cave in the late afternoon to get the best lighting on the incredible colors. Mariner's Cave is located at the northwestern end of Nuapapu Island and requires you to dive through an underwater entrance, surfacing in another grotto filled with turquoise light and, as with Swallows, the best time is the late afternoon.

Plan to dine on board, since the only real restaurants are at the starting and ending point of Neiafu, although you may find that a Tongan feast has been arranged by the charter company at one of the islands. This won't be the spectacle found in Hawaii, but the real thing, with Tongan delicacies such as lobster, fish, pork, papaya, bananas, coconuts and the staple of yam. More importantly, the Tongans are genuinely friendly, and their enthusiasm for song and dance is contagious.

Weather: Remember that Tonga is below the equator, so the seasons are reversed, with the coolest weather (and the shortest days) being in July and August when the temperatures average 65°-75°. For most of the year, however, you can expect midday highs in the 80s, and lows in the 70s. Hurricane season is from January through March, but they are forecast with good warnings. Because the months of June through August are the southern winter, the charter companies are often busy with bookings from Australians getting away to a warm climate, and the prime charter season spans from April through November.

NEW ZEALAND

New Zealand provides spectacular chartering opportunities, and it's no surprise that the country has more boats per capita than any other nation including the Scandinavian countries and the United Kingdom.

The Bay of Islands is certainly the most popular destination for both locals and foreign sailors, and is located at the eastern tip of North Island, known locally as Northland. At 35°S, the area has a mild subtropical climate and this protected bay holds literally hundreds of uninhabited islands. Within a 45-mile stretch of coastline, there are 86 islands and a handful of charter companies that serve the area. Opua and Russell are the two main charter bases, and both are set

New Zealand's Bay of Islands provides cruising in a protected island chain as well as opportunities for hiking and exploring ashore.

nearly in the center of a cruising area that extends from the village of KeriKeri in the west to Cape Brett at the east, although longer charters sometimes explore outside those boundaries. The scenery is delightful, with fertile green pastures rolling down to white beaches edged by emerald water that is clear enough to check your anchor.

The Bay of Islands Maritime and Historic Park is a preserve that keeps the islands in a pristine state, and local sailors take pride in the spotless condition. A garbage barge is provided at the southeast end of Motorua during the summer season and, at the southwest end of this same island, a buoy holds a water hose from a freshwater stream for the free use of cruising sailors. Motorua also has nature trails marked for flora and fauna, and you can stroll through the stands of pine and plunge into a cool tropical forest filled with giant ponga ferns. Pipi Bay is named after the clam-like bivalves that are found a few inches below the surface of the sand (look for tiny air bubbles) and then steamed and dipped in a garlic-butter broth. Throughout the islands, the diving and snorkeling is superb.

Te Hue Bay, which means Assassination Cove after the Maoris massacred early French explorers for violating their sacred areas, is very sheltered and has a superb beach reached by crossing a spit of land. For world cruiser Eric Hiscock,

New Zealand's Bay of Islands remains wild and untouched for the most part, providing ideal cruising grounds in pleasant conditions.

Protected and quiet anchorages are a trademark of New Zealand's Bay of Islands.

Opunga Cove was his favorite of this area, and the naturalized New Zealander would have known. On Motuarohia is a plaque commemorating Captain Cook's first explorations of the area, and the anchorages are overlooked by an ancient Maori fortress. Otehei Bay is another good anchorage that is well protected from the easterlies that come with rain, but it is often crowded with locals.

At the east end of the bay is Cape Brett, where you often encounter large swells rolling in unstopped from the South Pacific but, if the weather is settled, you can sail around the point and south to Whangamamumu Harbor, the site of an ancient whaling station. Above the pond is a lovely freshwater waterfall that the local sailors use as a natural shower and laundromat.

At the western end of the bay is KeriKeri, a delightful village noted for citrus products and on the way into the long cove are several lovely bays, the best of which is Opito. Once at KeriKeri, you need to watch the tides but you can enjoy the pubs, stores and local residents. KeriKeri Radio, by the way, produces a useful chart showing all the good anchorages and marine facilities in the Bay of Islands. If you don't get one with your boat, you can pick it up at most shops or chandleries.

At Russell is the Park Visitor's Center, which has an interesting audio-visual presentation on the islands, as well as waterside taverns once filled with whalers and now retaining the flavor of those wilder days.

While the Bay of Islands has reaped most of the publicity for chartering, the Hauraki Gulf near Auckland is the country's most active sailing area, and also the location of several charter companies. The water gateway to Auckland, the entire area is preserved as the Hauraki Gulf Maritime Park and there are dozens of lovely anchorages both north and south of Auckland. In addition, there are an array of islands, many uninhabited, and pretty beaches. The scenery is varied, ranging from rugged cliffs to rolling pastures and forests, and the entire Gulf is well-protected from all conditions except northers.

Across the Hauraki Gulf is the Coromandel peninsula, and the city of the same name was once a gold-rush boom town but is now a quiet village surrounded by abandoned mines. Nearby Te Kouma Harbour is a better protected overnight anchorage, however. Port Fitzroy on nearby Great Barrier Island is a delight, with numerous smaller bays that offer either solitude or quaint villages where you can dine on mussels and Steinlager.

The largest island is Waiheke, roughly 10 miles east of Auckland, and it has good protection from the prevailing southwesterlies in anchorages such as Omaru, Little Muddy and Man O'War Bay.

Both the Bay of Islands and the Hauraki Gulf are well charted with few hazards, and both have a well-maintained European buoyage system.

Weather: The best sailing season is from the end of October through mid-May during the southern spring, summer and fall. Most New Zealanders do their cruising from December through

February, so the anchorages are busier in those months when the daytime temperatures are in the mid-80s and the breezes are in the 10-15 knot range. The New Zealand winter, from June through September, has cooler temperatures and stronger winds.

AUSTRALIA

A land mass the size of the continental United States, Australia has a number of charter opportunities, but there are two areas that seem to draw both the locals and the foreigners time after time.

The Whitsundays off the Queensland coast are a chain of 97 islands so named by the ubiquitous Captain Cook aboard *Endeavour* in 1770 because he arrived on Whitsunday. Rocky but forested with pine and eucalyptus, they are protected from the ocean swells by the Great Barrier Reef and, as Captain Cook noted, the area is "one continued safe harbour." Literally an inland sea behind the protective Great Barrier Reef, there are hundreds of lovely anchorages and beaches within short sails of each other, and the area has been called a "Down-Under Virgin Islands" for both the choices and the pleasant conditions.

Shute Harbour and Airlie Beach on the mainland are the starting point for many charters (although there are companies based at Pioneer Bay, Abel Point and at Hamilton Island) because it lies within a 15-mile radius of the heart of the best cruising area. Except for a handful of resorts, the islands have been maintained in a natural state as a national park, and the only improvements are a few barbecue pits, trash barrels and moorings.

It would take several weeks to even superficially explore most of the islands, and charterers uniformly complain that they didn't have enough time. The best advice from local sailors is to simply relax, enjoy four or five good anchorages during a one-week charter, and come back for the rest.

Most charterers head for Palm Bay or Happy Bay after they check out the boats and stow their gear, since these good anchorages are just an hour's sail from Shute, and both have moorings provided by the local resorts so you don't have to worry about anchoring on the first night.

Nara Inlet, a steep-walled slash into Hook Island, is said to be the best anchorage in the Whitsundays (watch for the cockatoos in the trees), and the island also has the highest peak at 1478 feet. Herds of goats once roamed the island, placed there to help shipwrecked sailors survive but, today, you'll find the aborigine cave paintings more interesting, since they are more than 8000 years old.

The north side of Hook is a seemingly endless string of pretty bays with perfect coral reefs for diving and snorkeling, and Butterfly Bay is one of the most interesting. Watch for coral heads on the entry, and then row to the head of the bay where the creek leads to a rocky pool of fresh water shaded by trees that are often filled with butterflies.

Whitsunday Island, the largest island in the chain, has Whitehaven Beach at the east end. This is a three-mile stretch of squeaky white sand that is 99% silica rather than the usual beach of fine coral fragments, and is easily one of the most beautiful beaches in the world. Bareboat charters aren't allowed to explore the Great Barrier Reef, but floatplanes land at Whitehaven Beach to pick up anyone who wants to fly across for a couple of hours of snorkeling or reef walking. Several bays on the south side of Whitsunday Island, such as Turtle Bay, also have excellent coral reefs but aren't suitable for overnighting when the tradewinds are blowing.

If civilization appeals to you, you can radio ahead for a marina berth at Hamilton Island, the largest island development on the Australian coast. With its high rise resort, jet airport and bustling atmosphere of restaurants and bars, it's a startling counterpoint to the otherwise untouched Whitsundays.

Keep in mind the tides in the Whitsundays, since some of the narrow passages between islands can become maelstroms when a 5-6 knot current is running opposite the wind. Tidal range averages 12 feet, although it can reach 18 feet during spring tides, so anchor accordingly. You'll also need to plan ahead at some inlets, where the water may shoal at low water when the tide can drop 10-12 feet. Be prepared for *bullets*, the Aussie term for blasts of wind funneled down the mountain slopes and seemingly aimed directly at you when you're trying to set your anchor.

Australian regulations limit the maximum number of people aboard a bareboat charter yacht to eight, regardless of the number of berths the yacht may have. Anchoring is important because of the currents and tradewinds, so hone your skills before you set sail. As an added safety factor, all charterers are required to check in daily by VHF. Navigation is straightforward, the islands are well-charted, and the clear water makes eyeball navigation easy. Don't forget to look at the night sky, where you'll see the Southern Cross.

Weather: Lying about 20°S, the Whitsundays are balmy in winter and hot in summer. The charter season is from May through October, although you can charter year around. The windiest months are April to August when the southeast tradewinds blow steadily, and the rainy months are January to March, when there is also the chance of cyclones. December through April are the summer months, but September is recommended by locals as uncrowded. Water temperatures range from 79° in April to 72° in July.

Almost within sight of Sydney is a second charter area that is popular with Australians but overlooked by most overseas visitors. The Pittwater/Hawkesbury waterways are not far from Sydney's northern limits, but the timber-covered hills and spectacular sandstone cliffs (and their status as a national park) have resisted all development.

This is powerboat charter country, and you have three national parks to cruise through, including what the Aussies call a foreshore with the Hawkesbury River feeding an immense

The eerie rock formations of James Bond Island in Thailand's Phangnga Bay is where the 007 film Man With the Golden Gun *was made.*

estuary. In many areas, there are guest moorings, a necessity because of the often deep water. The Pittwater arm of this cruising area has Scotland Island at the south end, and beaches along the eastern shore.

The Hawkesbury River leads more than 50 miles inland, and you wind through high cliffs, forests, pleasant villages and uninhabited islands. Cowan Water lies west of the Hawkesbury River, and has a handful of coves with moorings and even a waterfall. All of this is just half an hour from downtown Sydney by commuter train, and a handful of charter companies offer powerboats of all shapes and sizes.

THAILAND

If there is one area that I would pick as the newest charter hot spot, it would have to be Thailand, which defines the word *foreign* for most visitors. On the way to your charter base, you may drive by jeep through cool green rubber plantations, past golden Buddhist temples, around water buffalo lounging in the road, and along some of the most incredibly beautiful coastline in the world. Once called Siam and the setting for *The King and I*, Thailand is a new addition to the international charter world.

I've never seen such perfect sand beaches, and most of them are not only

Thailand's Phangnga Bay is fast becoming a popular charter destination since it remains relatively untouched and pristine.

empty, but devoid of the human contamination found elsewhere in a world filled with beer bottles and Styrofoam cups. The rock formations found in Phangnga Bay defy description. Thailand has been compared to the Caribbean of Hemingway's time: untouched and absolutely enticing. When you anchor, you can look down in 60 feet of water and clearly see the shackle on your anchor. Local fishermen offer to share their catches of fish and lobster with you, and are embarrassed when you insist that they take a few cans of cola in return for the pet-sized lobsters.

Thailand is not as close as the Caribbean, of course, which has served to dissuade all but a few crewed charter yachts from venturing into these waters until recently, when both European and American bareboat charter companies have set up bases.

Located in the Andaman Sea at the southern end of the Thai peninsula leading to Malaysia, the island of Phuket (pronounced poo ket) is a growing Asian tourist resort with the usual beach-front condos, tourist shops, noisy motorbikes and late-night discos. But the offshore regions, with a few exceptions, have been left undiscovered except by the local fishermen and the few cruising sailors passing through the area.

Sunset over a yacht at anchor off Thailand.

Phangnga Bay east of Phuket is an eerie experience with hundreds of huge limestone pillar-islands that rise sheer from the surface of the sea. In mid-bay, these bizarre geologic monuments are in every direction, fading into the haze like an Oriental watercolor painting. The setting for the 007 film *Man With the Golden Gun*, there is now a James Bond Island that is usually overrun by tourist boats, but the rest of the bay remains untouched and protected. Areas in these towering islands are notched with caves, and the Thai collect swallows' nests from them for bird's nest soup, using rickety bamboo scaffoldings.

Deep water surrounds these islands and charts are good, so you can explore this area to your heart's content, perhaps even finding some of the hollow islands where caves lead into silent inner lagoons. At the north end of the bay is Ko Pan Yia, a Muslim settlement with its own mosque, shops and restaurants, all on stilts over the water. Further south at Chao Lai, you'll encounter the sea gypsies who live off the sea aboard their boats.

The Similan Islands, 50 miles west of Phuket in the Andaman Sea, are a chain of nine large and small government-protected gems with lush forests and rounded boulders reminiscent of those at The Baths in Virgin Gorda. The brilliant tropical fish seem to know they are protected, as they swim right up to peer into your face mask, and the soft white beaches are empty.

On a recent crewed powerboat charter in Thailand, I found myself sitting every evening in the cockpit as blue-white slashes of lightning flashed across the distant skies over the mountains. During the afternoons, towering pillars of cumulo-nimbus had grown into crennelated towers above the overheated mainland. After dark, the air was still and balmy in our quiet anchorages, and the only sound was the wavelets shushing onto the white sand beach. With an icy Singha beer on the teak armrest, it was a spectacular light show.

In addition to the Similan Islands, there are another three dozen islands scattered along the Thai coast, as well as the Phi Phi Islands to the southeast with their teeming marine life that attracts scuba divers. To the north, the islands of Surin are equally idyllic. Ko Racha Yai, just south of Phuket, has a marvelous deepwater cove with water so still that it reflects millions of tropical stars.

Just as spectacular as the scenery is the absence of other yachts. In fact, on my last charter in Thailand, we had four days without seeing another boat of any kind.

Ashore, the Thai cuisine combines seafood, meat and vegetables with coconut milk, lime, hot chilis and an array of spices into meals that are unique in the world. Be wary of green curries unless you have a leather palate. Local restaurants often don't bother with menus, and simply serve what was caught live that afternoon.

Racers can get into the action in Thailand during the Andaman Sea Race, a 60-miler from Phi Phi to Phuket in early December, or the King's Cup series of buoy races in mid-December.

Weather: The prime season for Phuket and the Andaman Sea runs roughly from November through April, when the northeast breezes blow steadily, the humidity is reduced, and there is virtually no rain. For the Gulf of Thailand, the season runs from January through August. The summer monsoon season, with daily rain and high humidity, lasts from June through October, and mid-summer months have a threat of typhoons. Temperatures remain in the 80° to 90° range year around.

Appendix 1: Charter Seasons

Location	Best Season	Comments
North America & Caribbean		
Bahamas	December-March	June-September have high humidity; strong northers blow January-April
Baja California	November-May	Summer is very hot; fall is hurricane season
Caribbean	Mid-December-March	The best winds are April-July; hurricanes possible July-October
Chesapeake	Mid-April to October spring and fall best	Mid-summer has light wind and thunderstorms
Florida	January-May	June-September are hot and humid
Great Lakes	June-September	Crowded in July
Maine	June-September	August is foggy
Northeast	May-October	Light summer winds
Pacific Northwest	June-September spring and fall best	Crowded in mid-summer
Sacramento Delta	May-October	
Southern California	Year-around	Crowded in summer
Europe		
British Isles	May-September	Expect rain
Greece	Spring and fall	Crowded in summer; meltemi winds blow regularly
Mediterranean	April-October	Summer months are crowded with tourists
Scandinavia	May-September	Long daylight hours
Turkey	Fall and spring	Summer is hot and windy
Western Europe	May-September	Expect rain

Pacific and Asia

Australia	May-October	Summer is wet and unstable
French Polynesia	March-November	November-April is humid and warm
New Zealand	Year around, but high season is October-May	June-September are windy and cooler; December-February are crowded
Thailand	November-April	Summer is humid, rainy, and typhoon season
Tonga	April-November	January-March is hurricane season

Appendix 2: Checklists

1. BAREBOAT CHECK-OUT LIST

Checking out on an unfamiliar charter yacht can be useful or frustrating, and the following list offers some suggestions for the information you need to enjoy a pleasant and safe charter:

Deck

- Anchor windlass operation, amount of rode and chain aboard
- Location of spare anchor, emergency windlass procedures
- Location and number of docklines and fenders
- Location of extra blocks, lines, winch handles, etc.
- Operation of bimini top and cockpit table

Safety

- Location of all life jackets, flares, fire extinguishers
- Location and use of boarding ladder and man-overboard equipment
- Operation and location of manual and automatic bilge pumps
- Location and installation of emergency tiller
- Test all flash and spotlights

Mechanical

- Location of all thru-hull fittings and operation of seacocks
- Location of batteries, operation of battery switches
- Operation of head and shower sump pump
- Proper methods of checking oil and water in engine
- Recommended rpm, oil pressure, water temperature
- Understand all switches and gauges on instrument panel
- Fuel tank capacity, location of deckplate filler
- Check operation of all lights and location of spare bulbs

Galley

- Have proper operation of stove demonstrated
- Location of spare stove fuel cannisters and change-over procedure
- Proper operation of refrigerator/freezer
- Capacity of water tank, valves for switching tanks, location of deckplate for filling water tank

Dinghy

- Operation of outboard, proper fuel and oil mixtures, spare shear pin
- Location of oars, bailer, fuel tank
- If inflatable, locate inflation pump

Navigation

- Location of all charts and cruising guides
- Proper documentation and ship's papers for customs clearance
- Proper use of radio (what channel charter company monitors, channel and time of local weather broadcasts)

General

- How does dinette convert to berth?
- Location and count of linens and towels

External

- Check condition of hull, rubrails, mast and rigging. Note in writing on check-out sheet any gouges or other damage to prevent being charged later.
- If possible, raise main and unfurl jib at dock to examine condition
- Confirm count of winch handles and location

2. DAILY CHECKLIST

Each day, you should prepare your charter yacht for use and, just as a pilot goes through a pre-flight checklist, the following is a minimum list for a pre-sail inspection:

Engine pre-start

- Check oil level, coolant level, belts
- Run blower
- Fuel level—note amount used daily

Warmed engine

- Monitor oil pressure, coolant temp, charging rate
- Water coming from exhaust

Bilges

- Check and pump dry daily

Fresh water

- Check and record amount used daily

Stove fuel

- Check and record daily

Anchor readiness

- Make sure primary anchor is ready for instant use

Deck

- Put away or secure all loose cushions
- Stow all personal belongings, such as books, hats, etc.

Below

- Close all hatches and ports until at sea
- Stow all gear that may fall when boat heels
- Make sure all lockers and drawers are secured shut

Further Reading

GENERAL

Handbook of Offshore Cruising, *Jim Howard*

Harbors of Enchantment, *Cynthia Kaul*

World Cruising Handbook, *Jimmy Cornell*

SEAMANSHIP

The Annapolis Book of Seamanship, *John Rousmaniere*

SAFETY/FIRST AID

Advanced First Aid Afloat, *Peter F. Eastman*, M.D.

Your Offshore Doctor, *Michael H. Beilan*, M.D.

WEATHER

Sailor's Weather Guide, *Jeff Markell*

CARIBBEAN

Caribbean Cruising Handbook, *Bill Robinson*

Cruising Guide to the Caribbean and Bahamas, *William Stone* and *Ann Hayes*

Cruising Guide to the Eastern Caribbean (4 volumes), *Don Street*

Cruising Guide to the Leeward Islands, *Cruising Guide Publications*

Cruising Guide to the Virgin Islands, *Nancy* and *Simon Scott*

Exploring the Windward Islands, *Cruising Guide Publications*

Sailor's Guide to the Windward Islands, *Cruising Guide Publications*

Street's Cruising Guides (various editions), *Don Street*

Yachtsman's Guide to the Virgin Islands, *Harry Klein*

Yachtsman's Guide to the Windward Islands, *Julius Wilensky*

BAHAMAS AND NORTH AMERICA

Bahamas

Bahama Islands, *Rigg/Kline*

Cruising Guide to the Bahamas, *Julius Wilensky*

Yachtsman's Guide to the Bahamas, *Harry Kline*

Florida

Cruising Guide to Eastern Florida, *Claiborne S. Young*

Cruising Guide to the Florida Keys, *Capt. Frank Papy*

Cruising Guide to Western Florida, *Claiborne S. Young*

The Intracoastal Waterway, *Jan* and *Bill Moeller*

Waterway Guide, Southern edition

Chesapeake

Waterway Guide, Mid-Atlantic edition

Cruising Guide to the Chesapeake, *Stone, Blanchard* and *Hayes*

New England

Cruising Guide to Maine (2 volumes), *Don Johnson*

Cruising Guide to the New England Coast, *Robert Duncan, John P. Ware* and *Wally Finn*

Great Lakes

Gunkholer's Guide to the North Channel, *P.* and *J. Nerbonne*

The Ports Cruising Guide to Georgian Bay and the North Channel

Waterways Guide, Great Lakes edition

Well-Favored Passage, *Marjorie Cahn*

Baja California

Sea of Cortez Guide, *Dix Brow*

California

Cruising Guide to California's Channel Islands, *Brian Fagan*

Cruising the Delta, *Hal Schell*

Dawdling on the Delta, *Hal Schell*

Pacific Northwest

Cruising the San Juan Islands, *Bruce Calhoun*

Gunkholing in the San Juan Islands, *Jo Bailey* and *Carl Nyberg*

Northwest Passages, *Bruce Calhoun*

The San Juan Islands, Afoot and Afloat, *Marge* and *Ted Mueller*

EUROPE

Greece

The Aegean: A Sea Guide, *H.M. Denham*

Greek Waters Pilot, *Rod Heikell*

Mediterranean

Italian Waters Pilot, *Rod Heikell*

Mediterranean Cruising Handbook, *Rod Heikell*

South France Pilot, *Robin Brandon*

Turkey

Cruising Guide to the Turquoise Coast of Turkey, *Marcia Davock*

Turkey and the Dodecanese Cruising Pilot, *Robin Petherbridge*

Turkish Waters Pilot, *Rob Heikell*

British Isles

The Channel Handbooks, *R.M. Bowker*

Cruising Association Handbook

The Macmillan & Silk Cut Nautical Almanac, *Klaus Boehm*

Scottish West Coast Pilot, *Mark Brackenbury*

South England Pilot, *Robin Brandon*

Norway

Norwegian Cruising Guide, *John Armitage* and *Mark Brackenbury*

South Pacific and Asia

Boating Guide to the New South Wales South Coast, *Jeff Toghill*
Cruising Guide to French Polynesia, *Fred Boehme*
Cruising Guide to New Zealand's Bay of Islands, *Rainbow Yacht Charters*
Cruising Guide to Tahiti and the French Society Islands, *Marcia Davock*
Landfalls of Paradise, *Earl R. Hinz*
New Zealand's Bay of Islands: The Land and Sea Guide, *Claire Jones*
Thailand: Sail Thailand

Index

Abacos, 105, 160, 161
Airline reservations, 79
Anchoring, 40, 49, 80, 93-102
Anguilla, 148, 151, 152
Annapolis, 164
Antigua, 153
Apostle Islands, 20, 80, 167
Arrival time, 28
Aruba, 148
Australia, 198-200

Bahamas, 20, 23, 39, 159-162
Bahamas mooring, 102, 160
Baja California, 15, 20, 21, 56, 166, 167-168
Barbecues, 141
Baths, Virgin Gorda, 150
Bay of Islands, 194
Belize, 21, 148
Bequia, 156
Bites and stings, 125
Bitter End Yacht Club, 150
Bonaire, 148
Booking charters, 65
Breakdowns, 28
British Isles, 182-186
British Virgin Islands, 3, 5, 57, 71, 149-150
Bugs, 142

Cameras, 75-76
Cancellations, 67
Cane Garden Bay, 151
Caneel Bay, 151
Canouan Island, 156
Caribbean, 4, 23, 28, 103, 105, 107, 108, 131, 147-158
Caribbean Sailing Yachts, 31
Carriacou, 158
Cary, Charlie and Ginny, 32
Catalina Island, 168
Catamarans, 39, 45-49
Charlotte Amalie, 149, 151
Charter
- check-in, 71
- check-out, 86-87
- contract, 70
- costs, 21
- inventory, 70
- seasons, 148, 205

Checklists, 207
Chesapeake Bay, 163-164
Children, 138-139
Christmas winds, 148
Clearance papers, 142-143
Clothing, 74-75
Collisions, 121
Crew overboard, 117-118
Crewed charters, 7
Cruz Bay, 151
Curaçao, 148

Denmark, 187-188
Departure time, 28
Deposits, 65-66
Dinghies, 41, 109-115
Docking, 88
Dominica, 148, 151, 153
Dutch Windwards, 148

Educational charters, 11
English Harbour, 153
Europe, 99, 175-188
Exumas, 160, 162

Finland, 186
Fire, 118-119
First aid, 123-125
Flags, 143
Flooding, 120
Florida Keys, 80, 162-163
Flotilla charters, 8-9
Fort Lauderdale, 162
France, 182
French Antilles, 148
French Polynesia, 189-193
Fuel, 80

Galápagos, 11
Galleys, 40, 54
Garbage, 142
Generators, 139
Gorda Sound, 150
Great Lakes, 165, 167
Greater Antilles, 147-148
Greece, 131, 175-178
Grenada, 148, 155, 158
Grenadines, 148, 155-158
Guadeloupe, 148, 151, 153
Gulf Islands, 172
Gustavia, 152-153

Head boats, 11
Heavy weather, 89-90
Hotels, 80
Hurricanes, 148

Insurance, 67-69
Ireland, 185-186

Jost Van Dyke, 151

Key West, 163
Knots, 90-91

Lake Superior, 20
Leeward Islands, 148, 151-155
Lesser Antilles, 148
Logbook, 70-71
Long Island Sound, 165

Maine, 165
Marigot, 151, 155
Marsh Harbour, 160, 161
Martinique, 148, 155
Mayreau, 157
Mediterranean, 21, 105, 178-181
Mediterranean mooring, 99-102, 153
Menus, 135
Miami, 159, 162
Michener, James, 155
Money, 143-144
Moorings, 88
Moorings, The, 4, 5, 6, 11, 25, 27, 28, 32, 69, 71, 150
Mustique, 155, 156

Navigation, 103-108
Netherlands, 182
New Zealand, 194-198
Norman Island, 150
Northeastern U.S., 164
Norway, 21, 188

Outboards, 110, 114

Pacific Northwest, 15, 19, 25, 28, 171-173
Packing, 74
Penmar Marine, 25
Philipsburg, 151
Phuket, 57, 200
Power charters, 51-59
Prickly Pear Cays, 152

Privacy, 38, 137-138
Propellers, 121
Provisioning, 21, 81, 127-135

Red Hook Bay, 151
Refrigerators, 140
Rhone, 150
Road Bay, 152
Road Town, Tortola, 150
Rolex Cup, 158
Running aground, 119-120

Saba, 148, 153
Sacramento Delta, 169-171
Sailing schools, 9-10, 29
Salt Island, 150
San Juan Islands, 80, 171-173
Scandinavia, 105, 186-188
Scotland, 13, 20, 131, 183-185
Seamanship, 85-91
Seasickness, 78, 124-125
Seasons, 80
Security deposit, 67
Sir Francis Drake Channel, 150
Snorkel gear, 75, 81
Soper's Hole, 151
South Pacific , 131, 189-194
Southern California, 168-169
St. Barthelemy, 148, 151-153
St. Eustatius, 148, 153
St. John, 151
St. Kitts, 151
St. Maarten/ St. Martin, 5, 24, 131, 148, 151, 153
St. Vincent, 148, 155
Stardust Charters, 32
Statia, 148, 153
Stevenson, Robert Louis, 150
Stowage, 140-141
Sunburn, 123-124
Sunglasses, 76
Sunsail Charters, 11, 32, 41
Sweden, 186-187

Tahiti, 3, 9, 189-193
Taxes, 21
Thailand, 79, 200-203
Tobago Cays, 149, 156
Toilets, 141-142
Tonga, 193-194
Tortola, 149
Turkey, 79, 181-182

Union Island, 158
U.S. Coast Guard, 29

Van Ost, John, 31
Venezuela, 148
Ventilation, 39
Virgin Gorda, 150
Virgin Islands, 19, 20, 80, 148, 149-151

Water, 39-40, 139-140
Whitsunday Islands, 198
Windward Islands, 148, 155

Other books of interest from Sheridan House

THE PERFECT FIRST MATE

A WOMAN'S GUIDE TO RECREATIONAL BOATING

by Joy Smith

"In this gem of a book, a seasoned cruiser offers tips on interpersonal relationships afloat."

John Rousmaniere, SailNet.com

BASIC COASTAL NAVIGATION

AN INTRODUCTION TO PILOTING FOR SAIL AND POWER

by Frank Larkin

"An excellent self-teaching textbook… His approach is straightforward and his sense of humor refreshing."

The Ensign

IF *THE SHOE* FITS

by Rae Ellen Lee

"… a wonderful saga, a fantasy come true for many armchair sailors, told from the viewpoint of a reluctant first mate with a candid and humorous perspective."

Publishers Weekly

HANDBOOK OF OFFSHORE CRUISING

THE DREAM AND REALITY OF MODERN OCEAN CRUISING

by Jim Howard

revised and updated by Charles J. Doane

Since this book was first published in 1994, it has established itself as *the* most complete, most reliable and most-read guide for those planning to sail across the oceans.

THE *SAIL* BOOK OF COMMONSENSE CRUISING

edited by Patience Wales

As a regular feature of *SAIL* Magazine, "Commonsense Cruising" has become the most popular column. Practical advice is given on numerous aspects of cruising, and is presented with a good dose of common sense. A must for every sailor.